045

D1395084

'Richard Foster diagnoses this generation's major threat to the mature life in Christ as distraction. In response he does again what he does so well: tunnels to the roots of our deep-rooted ancestors and makes us firsthand participants in the church's practice of a life of meditative prayer.'

Eugene Peterson

'This is Richard Foster at his best – describing the inner life with clarity and wisdom gained from his own experience. The content of this book, as experienced through his teaching, changed my life thirty years ago, opening me to a real, vibrant relationship with God through silence and listening. Over time this teaching has matured, and is destined to become a classic. If you want to experience an intimate relationship with God, simply read this book and put it into practice. Heaven awaits!'

James Bryan Smith

Also by Richard J. Foster

Sanctuary of the Soul

A journey into meditative prayer

RICHARD J. FOSTER

HODDER &
STOUGHTON

Unless indicated otherwise, Scripture quotations are taken from the Holy
Bible, New Revised Standard Version. Copyright © 1989 by the Division of
Christian Education of the National Council of Churches in the USA. Used
by permission. All rights reserved.

First published in Great Britain in 2011 by Hodder & Stoughton
An Hachette UK company

1

A CIP catalogue record for this title is available from the British Library.

ISBN 978 1 444 70257 6
eBook ISBN 978 1 444 70262 0

Printed and bound in the UK by Clays Ltd, St Ives plc

Hodder & Stoughton policy is to use papers that are natural, renewable
and recyclable products and made from wood grown in sustainable forests.
The logging and manufacturing processes are expected to conform to the
environmental regulations of the country of origin.

Hodder & Stoughton Ltd
338 Euston Road
London NW1 3BH

www.hodderfaith.com

To William Luther Vaswig
Man of Prayer
Best friend

Contents

A Beginning Word

Meditation is the tongue of the soul
and the language of our spirit.
JEREMY TAYLOR

JESUS CHRIST IS ALIVE AND HERE to teach his people himself. His voice is not hard to hear; his vocabulary is not difficult to understand. But learning to listen well and to hear correctly is no small task.

My first conscious experience of hearing the voice of Jesus occurred when I was a college student. It grew out of a period of genuine frustration. Because of my poor academic training and a less-than-stellar intellect, it seemed I had to study harder than everyone else if I was to succeed in college. On top of that I was carrying two part-time jobs to bring in enough money to put food on the table and to buy books. My first job was at a cannery on the cleanup crew after the night shift. I worked from four to six each morning steam-cleaning the machinery, and I got back to the college just in time to wash dishes at the dining commons, my second job.

It was a perfect schedule, for I could do all of this before my first class began at eight a.m. Then at lunch and supper I washed dishes again, which allowed me to eat at the dining commons. In those days many students complained about the food service at the college . . . but not me. Both of my parents had been ill and died earlier, so my two brothers and I lived on whatever we could scrape together. For me college dining food was banquet fare.

In addition to the work and study I, together with a good college friend, had formed a ministry effort with the rather quaint title of "Youth Accent." This ministry work took us to churches each weekend, where between us we would speak five or six times from Friday evening to Sunday noon, after which we would jump in the car and make our way back to the campus. Then too I was doing some service work at a local church . . . oh, and I was involved in student government . . . all of which made for a heavy load for a young college sophomore. Still, I believed each of these tasks was important for several reasons: to earn needed money, to hone my speaking skills and to interact with the lives of precious people. But they left little time for the leisure and social activities that seemed to be such a large part of other students' lives. And I was frustrated at my seeming loss.

One evening I was taking a stretch break from study, walking out into the night. Soon I began speaking prayers of complaint . . . a little like the lament psalms in the Bible. I wasn't angry, really, just frustrated. They were "poor me" kinds of prayers. My walking took me into a nearby woods and, as I walked along by the light of the moon, my complaining prayers began to diminish and I became more and more quiet. Finally, I fell into total silence. A still, listening silence. It was then that God spoke, spoke out of the stillness and into my frustration.

You know how we are able to distinguish between human speakers by the quality of their voice, the spirit in their voice and, of course, the content of what is being said? It is much the same with the divine voice. The quality of God's voice is one of drawing and encouraging. The spirit in God's voice is all grace and mercy. And the content of what is being said is always consistent with what God has said before—we have a huge biblical witness upon which to test our leadings. Now, I am not speaking here of an outward voice that can be captured by electronic equipment. That no doubt is possible, as the Bible gives ample witness. But here I am speaking of an inward whisper, a deep speaking into the heart, an interior knowing.

"You are frustrated and sorry for yourself," God seemed to be saying. "Sorry for yourself because you do not have all your desires satisfied. But if you will be *with me* you do not have to have all your desires satisfied. *With me* is ultimate and complete satisfaction. If you are genuinely *with me* you are in the best place possible."

That was all. No promise to transform my life circumstances. No guarantee of wealth and prosperity and all my worldly desires. No pledge to change a single thing. And yet those words quietly dissipated my frustration and overcame my self-pity. I walked out of the woods with a fresh spring in my step. I had been addressed personally, intimately. The voice of the true Shepherd was altogether sufficient.

※　　※　　※

In the pages that follow we will seek to explore more fully what it means to experience the divine whisper for ourselves. How does God speak to us? What should we expect . . . or even hope for? Are there conditions of heart and mind that open us to God's loving—and terrifying—voice? How can we develop an inward, prayer-filled listening? It is questions like these and more that we will explore.

To conclude each of the three major parts of this book I share an extended personal experience that I hope will illustrate and expand on what I have been sharing with you. I call these elements "Entering the Experience," for I do hope that my story will encourage you to enter into your own experiences of meditative prayer.

PART I

Laying the Foundation

Teach me to stop and listen,
Teach me to center down.
Teach me the use of silence,
Teach me where peace is found.

Teach me to hear Your calling,
Teach me to search Your Word.
Teach me to hear in silence,
Things I have never heard.

Teach me to be collected,
Teach me to be in tune,
Teach me to be directed,
Silence will end so soon.

Then when it's time for moving,
Grant it that I might bring,
To every day and moment,
Peace from a silent spring.

KEN MEDEMA

And Isaac went out to meditate in the field at the eventide.

GENESIS 24:63 KJV

God Speaking, Teaching and Acting

As fundamental a step as we can take . . . is learning to meditate
on Scripture—learning first to hear God's word, and let it
inform and take root in us. This may be extremely difficult, for
the churches have no courses on meditation, despite the fact that
it is an art that must be learned from those who have mastered it,
and despite the fact that the supreme task of the church is to
listen to the Word of God.

ELIZABETH O'CONNOR

OH, LET ME TELL YOU HOW MUCH God desires our presence. How much God longs to hear from us. How much God yearns to communicate with us. At the very heart of God is the passionate disposition to be in loving fellowship with you . . . with me. From the human side of this equation it is meditative prayer that ushers us into this divine-human fellowship.

A PLACE TO STAND
The biblical foundation for meditation is discovered in the

great reality of God speaking, teaching and acting that lies at the center of the scriptural witness. God brought the universe crashing into existence by the word of his command. God said, "Let there be light," and the big bang occurred.

In the Garden, Adam and Eve talked with God *and* God talked with them—they were in communion. Then came the Fall, and in an important sense the experience of perpetual communion was ruptured, for Adam and Eve hid from God. But God continued to reach out to his rebellious children, and in the stories of Cain and Abel, Noah and Abraham and so many others we see God speaking and acting, teaching and guiding.

Moses learned, albeit with many vacillations and detours, how to hear God's voice and obey God's word. In fact, Scripture witnesses that God spoke to Moses "face to face, as one speaks to a friend" (Ex 33:11). There was a sense of intimate relationship, of communion. As a people, however, the Israelites were not prepared for such intimacy. Once they learned a little about God, they realized that being in his presence was dangerous business and told Moses so: "You speak to us, and we will listen; but do not let God speak to us, or we will die" (Ex 20:19).

This marked the beginning of the great line of prophets and judges, Moses being the first. But it was a step away from the sense of God's immediacy, the sense of the cloud by day and the pillar of fire by night.

Then under Samuel the people clamored for a king. This disturbed Samuel greatly, but God told him not to be discouraged, "for they have not rejected you, but they have rejected me from being king over them" (1 Sam 8:7). Under Moses they rejected God's immediacy; under Samuel they rejected God's direct rule. "Give us a prophet, give us a king, give us a go-between so we do not have to come into God's presence for ourselves," they said. So it is today. We do not have to look at religion on the contemporary scene very deeply before we see that it is saturated with the dogma of the mediator. "Give us a pastor, give us a priest, give us someone who will do it for us so we can avoid intimacy with God ourselves and continue to reap the benefits," we say.

Still, in the fullness of time Jesus came and taught the present reality of the kingdom of God and demonstrated what life could be like in this kingdom. Jesus showed us God's yearning for the gathering of an all-inclusive community of loving persons with God himself at its heart as its prime Sustainer and most glorious Inhabitant. Jesus established a living fellowship that would know him as Redeemer and King, listening to him in all things and obeying him at all times.

Jesus in his intimate relationship with the Father modeled for us the reality of this life of constantly hearing and obeying. "The Son can do nothing on his own, but only what he sees the Father doing; for whatever the Father does, the Son does likewise" (Jn 5:19). "I can do nothing on my own. As I hear, I judge" (Jn 5:30). "The words that I say to you I do not speak on my own; but the Father who dwells in me does his works" (Jn 14:10). When Jesus told his disciples to abide in him, they could understand what he meant, for he was abiding in the Father. Jesus declared (and continues to declare to us today) that he is the good Shepherd and that his sheep know his voice (Jn 10:4). He made it clear that the Comforter would come, the Spirit of truth who would guide his people into all truth (Jn 16:13).

In his second volume Luke clearly implies that after the resurrection and ascension Jesus continues "to do and to teach," even though the people can no longer see him with the naked eye (Acts 1:1 NIV). Both Peter and Stephen point to Jesus as the fulfillment of the prophecy of Deuteronomy 18:15 that a prophet like Moses would arise who would speak and whom the people would hear and obey (Acts 3:22; 7:37).* In the book of Acts we see the resurrected and reigning Christ, through the Holy Spirit, teaching and guiding his children: leading Philip to new unreached cultures (Acts 8), revealing his messiahship to Paul (Acts 9), teaching Peter about his racial prejudices (Acts 10), guiding the believing fellowship out of its cultural captivity (Acts 15).

And the wonderful news is that Jesus has not stopped act-

---

*See also Deut 18:15-18; Mt 17:5; Jn 1:21; 4:19-25; 6:14; 7:37-40; Heb 1:1-13; 3:7-8; 12:25.

ing and speaking. He is resurrected and at work in our world. He is not idle. He is alive and among us as our Prophet to teach us, our Priest to forgive us, our King to rule us, our Shepherd to guide us, our Friend to come alongside us.

TWO ENRICHING WORDS

Two Hebrew words deeply inform and enrich our understanding of meditative prayer: *haga* and *siach*. Our English Bibles most often translate both of these words with the simple word "meditate." Actually these two Hebrew words convey a host of nuances: to mutter, to moan, to whisper, to reflect, to rehearse, to muse and even to coo like the dove (Is 59:11).

Often the emphasis of these words is on silent reflection upon God's works in nature (Ps 143:5; 145:5) or God's Word (Ps 119:15, 23, 27, 48, 78, 148). At other times it involves audible murmuring, especially when the object of our meditation is Torah, or the Law of God: "This book of the law shall not depart out of your mouth; you shall meditate on it day and night, so that you may be careful to act in accordance with all that is written in it" (Josh 1:8).

This passage from Joshua underscores a central element of the biblical view of meditation: obedience.* This is in

---

*Many of the passages that use the words *haga* (הָגָה) or *siach* (שִׂיחַ) carry with them this idea of obedience to the will and ways of God. See Ps 1:2; 49:3; 119:15; 119:48; 119:97; 119:99 and others.

marked contrast to the various forms of meditation in many religions around the world. The biblical stress is always on ethical change, character transformation, obedience to the Word of the Lord.

Philosopher Ken Bryson of Nova Scotia observes, "Old Testament meditation moves through silence to dwell on a spirituality of words, namely, the precepts, statutes, words, and commandments of the Torah." So in the biblical witness we have this dual nature of meditation on stillness and action. This is why I constantly seek to define Christian meditation in terms of "hearing and obeying." Always this double emphasis. On the one hand we are called to silence, to stillness, to quieting "creaturely activity," as the old writers often put it. On the other hand we are called to action, to right behavior, to obedience to the will and ways of God. Hearing and obeying. Always hearing and obeying. These are things we learn from *haga* and *siach*.

Oh, may our hearts and minds be saturated with the longing of the psalmist: "Let the words of my mouth and the meditation of my heart be acceptable to you, O LORD, my rock and my redeemer" (Ps 19:14).

BEYOND EARTHQUAKE, WIND AND FIRE

Elijah and his shattering experience in the cave at Mount Horeb might become for us something of a paradigm for meditation. A metaphor for listening prayer, if you will.

You may remember the story recorded for us in 1 Kings 18 and 19. How Elijah triumphed over the prophets of Baal at Mount Carmel. How Jezebel sought to kill him. How Elijah ran for his life. How, exhausted and frozen with fear, Elijah asked for death under the broom tree: "It is enough; now, O LORD, take away my life" (1 Kings 19:4). How the angel of the Lord touched Elijah and gave him a hearty breakfast . . . twice. How on the strength of those meals he journeyed forty days and forty nights until at last he came to Horeb, the mountain of God. And how he entered a cave and spent the night there . . . desolate, lonely, defeated.

You know, sometimes the pressures of my own life crowd in and I want to cry out, "Move over, Elijah. Let me crawl into your cave with you." Perhaps you too have known times of discouragement and depression and have wanted to join Elijah in his cave. Mount Horeb's cave is a place of despair, desolation and dejection.

But now we will see why Elijah's story on Mount Horeb is a metaphor for meditative prayer. God coaxes Elijah out of his cave of depression and onto the mountaintop: "Go out and stand on the mountain before the LORD, for the LORD is about to pass by" (1 Kings 19:11). Those words, "the LORD is about to pass by," call to mind another mountain—Sinai—where in dramatic fashion God met with Moses and gave forth what we today call the Ten Commandments. We remember the story well, of course . . . and so did Elijah. The burning bush. The tablets of stone cut by the finger of God. The fangs of lightning. Boulders split apart. Trees reduced to embers. Roaring winds and deafening thunder rolling out across the canyons. Then we remember—and so did Elijah—how Moses hid in the cleft of the rock as the Lord God, the Almighty, passed by in a heart-stopping display of divine glory.

And now, here on Mount Horeb, God is about to pass by Elijah. On Sinai God's presence came forth in a massive fireworks display of natural phenomena. On Horeb there were indeed ferocious winds, shattering earthquakes and scorching fires. But God was not in any of these things. This must have been a shock to Elijah. Nothing of God was in the earthquake, wind or fire. It was only after all of nature's fireworks passed away and there was perfect stillness that God came to Elijah in a still small Voice, in the divine Whisper, in "a sound of sheer silence" (1 Kings 19:12). The Lord speaks to Elijah not in the ferociousness of nature but in silence, in "the soft whisper of a voice" (1 Kings 19:12 TEV).

On the mountaintop Elijah stands in utter humility before God. His humility flows from a desperation seen in his terror of Jezebel and in his own desire to die. And it is in that humility of heart that Elijah hears the *debar Yahweh*, the word of the Lord. The poet John Greenleaf Whittier wrote:

Breathe through the heat of our desire Thy coolness
    and Thy balm;
    Let sense be dumb, let flesh retire;
Speak through the earthquake, wind, and fire,
    O still, small voice of calm.

Oh, may we in quiet humility adopt the heart of Elijah. May we with humility of heart heed the counsel of the psalmist: "Be still before the LORD, and wait patiently for him" (Ps 37:7).

You may remember that Elijah stood upon yet another mountain of God: Mount Hermon, the mountain of the transfiguration. There on Mount Hermon he stood alongside Moses—together representing the law and the prophets. There on that mountain they saw Jesus, the Christ, transfigured, "and his face shone like the sun, and his clothes became dazzling white" (Mt 17:2). There on that mountain Elijah and Moses carried on an intimate conversation with Jesus, experiencing the fulfillment of all they had longed for, dreamed for, worked for (Mt 17:3). What a conversation that must have been!

THE STORY CONTINUES ON

Since that moment, faithful disciples of Jesus for two millennia have witnessed to the reality of a with-God life, the reality of "our communicating Cosmos." How unfortunate that we today know so little of the vast sea of literature on

Christian meditation by faithful believers throughout the centuries! From Catholic to Protestant, from Eastern Orthodox to Western Free Church, we are urged to "live in his presence in uninterrupted fellowship." The Russian mystic Theophan the Recluse said, "To pray is to descend with the mind into the heart, and there to stand before the face of the Lord, ever-present, all seeing, within you." The twentieth-century Lutheran martyr Dietrich Bonhoeffer, when asked why he meditated, replied, "Because I am a Christian." The witness of Scripture and the witness of the devotional masters both invite us to experience, in the words of Madame Guyon, "the depths of Jesus Christ."

A Familiar Friendship with Jesus

True silence is a key to the immense
and flaming heart of God.
CATHERINE DE HUECK DOHERTY

*I*N MEDITATIVE PRAYER WE ARE growing into what
Thomas à Kempis called "a familiar friendship with Jesus."
We are learning to sink down into the light and life of
Christ and becoming comfortable in this posture. We experience the perpetual presence of the Lord ("omnipres-
ence," as we say) not just as theological dogma but as radiant reality. "He walks with me and he talks with me" ceases
to be pious jargon and instead becomes a straightforward
description of daily life.

Please understand me: I am not speaking of some mushy,
giddy, buddy-buddy relationship. Such insipid sentimental-
ity only betrays how little we know, how distant we are
from the Lord high and lifted up who is revealed to us in
Scripture. John tells us in his Apocalypse that when he saw

the reigning Christ he "fell at his feet as though dead" . . .
and so should we (Rev 1:17). The reality I speak of is akin
to what the disciples felt in the upper room when they experienced both intense intimacy and awe-full reverence.

AN INNER SANCTUARY IN THE HEART

In meditative prayer we are creating the emotional and
spiritual space that allows God to construct an inner sanctuary in the heart. The wonderful verse "Behold, I stand
at the door, and knock" was originally penned for believers, not unbelievers (Rev 3:20 KJV). Jesus is knocking at
the door of our heart—daily, hourly, moment by moment. He is longing to eat with us, to commune with us.
He desires a perpetual Eucharistic feast in the inner sanctuary of the heart. Jesus is knocking; meditative prayer
opens the door.

The wise apostle Paul reminds us that we are no longer
strangers and aliens to the divine fellowship. We have become members of the household of God, a household based
on the solid foundation of the apostles and prophets. Jesus
himself is the key cornerstone, and it is through him that
"the whole structure is joined together and grows into a
holy temple in the Lord; in whom you also are built together spiritually into *a dwelling place for God*" (Eph 2:21-22,
emphasis added).

Allow me to underscore that phrase: my heart, your

heart is being made into "a dwelling place for God."* Now, I do not know about you but if my heart is to become "a dwelling place of God," some major renovations are needed! Teresa of Avila, reflecting on the evil in her own heart, once prayed, "O my Lord, since it seems You have determined to save me, I beseech Your Majesty . . . don't You think it would be good . . . if the inn where You have to dwell continually would not get so dirty?"

All real formation work is "heart work," as the great Puritan divines dubbed it. The human heart is the wellspring of all human action. It is the center of all volition and the deep realities of the spirit. John Flavel, a seventeenth-century English Puritan, noted that the "greatest difficulty in conversion, is to win the heart *to* God; and the greatest difficulty after conversion, is to keep the heart *with* God. . . . Heart-work is hard work indeed."

Two Central Realities

As we consider the transformation of the human heart, we need to keep two central realities clearly in mind. To begin with, we simply cannot program our own heart. We cannot program anyone else's heart. There is a whole theology that stands behind these statements. I will not go into ex-

---

*Note also Paul's rather blunt statement to the Christian fellowship at Corinth: "Do you not know that you are God's temple and that God's Spirit dwells in you?" (1 Cor 3:16).

treme detail here; I will just state it in this flatfooted manner: You are not in charge of the transformation of your heart. Neither am I. This is God's domain, and you and I are utterly dependent on God to accomplish the work of heart transformation. We can want heart transformation and seek after heart transformation. Those certainly are good things to do. But the truth is we do not make transformation happen. God does.

Second, the human heart itself is part of our problem. We are, each and every one of us, a tangled mass of motives: hope and fear, faith and doubt, simplicity and duplicity, honesty and falsity, openness and guile. God knows our heart in ways we can never know. Supernatural abilities are needed to untangle the mess. God is the only one who can separate the true from the false. Only God can purify the motives of the heart.

So, you see, we are utterly, utterly dependent upon God to do this transforming work in us: the work of heart purity, of soul conversion, of inward formation, of life transformation. This solitary and interior work within the heart is the most important, the most real, the most lasting reality in human life.

Therefore, the devotional masters' constant appeal to heart purification speaks an important word for us. It is no vain thing for us to return to our first love over and over and over again. It is an act of faith to continually cry out to

God to search us and to know our heart and to root out every wicked way in us (Ps 139:23-24). This is a vital aspect of the salvation of the Lord.

Let me stress this central reality once again: God is the ultimate form-er and trans-former of the human heart. Having said this, I hasten to add that God has graciously invited you and me to participate in this highest, deepest work of heart transformation. Remember, God does not come uninvited. If certain chambers of our heart have never experienced God's healing touch, perhaps it is because we have never welcomed the divine Scrutiny.

ENTERING INTO HEART TRANSFORMATION

So, what does this formation work deep in the subterranean chambers of the heart look like?

From the divine side of the equation we can see only through a glass darkly. It is a glorious mystery, this working of God upon the human heart. Allowing maximum freedom and volition. Pursuing us quietly, relentlessly. Extending graces and mercies we do not deserve or even seek. Granting us quantum leaps forward into love, joy, peace, patience, kindness, goodness, faithfulness, gentleness and self-control. And so much more. This is *the great work,* but we are severely limited in what we can say about it or even understand. We can only stand in awe and doxology at the goodness of God.

But let me attempt to describe it for you from the human side of the equation. It begins first by our turning to the Light of Jesus. We "mind the Light," as the old writers put it. For some this is an excruciatingly slow turning, turning, till we turn round right. For others it is instantaneous and glorious. In either case we are coming to trust in Jesus, to accept Jesus as our Life. We are born from above, as we read in John 3.

But our being born from above, of necessity, includes our being formed from above. Being spiritually born is a beginning—a wonder-filled, glorious beginning. It is not an ending. Much intense formation work is necessary before we can stand the fires of heaven. Much training is necessary before we are the kind of person who can safely and easily reign with God.

So now, we are ushered into this new relationship. As Peter put it, we "have been born anew, not of perishable but of imperishable seed, through the living and enduring word of God" (1 Pet 1:23). God is alive! Jesus is real and active in our little affairs.

Hence we begin to pray, to enter into an interactive communication and communion with God. But in the beginning our praying is uneasy and halting. It's like an alternating current of electricity; our attention bounces back and forth from divine glories to the mundane tasks of daily life. Back and forth, back and forth. And often the alternating is worse—much worse—than not praying at all. One moment we are reveling in holy mysteries and the next moment our minds are wallowing in the gutter of carnal desires.

We feel fractured and fragmented. As Thomas Kelly put it, we are living in "an intolerable scramble of panting feverishness." We feel the pull and push of many obligations and we try to fulfill them all. And more often than not we find ourselves "unhappy, uneasy, strained, oppressed and fearful we shall be shallow."

Nevertheless, throughout our seeking and struggling we are continually doing three things:

1. We are asking. Always asking. "Change my heart, O God; make it ever true. Change my heart, O God; may I be like you." Asking, always asking.

2. We are listening. Always listening. Like Elijah, we wait through earthquake, wind and fire for the still, small Voice. Listening, always listening.

3. We are obeying. Always obeying. We obey Christ in all things. We obey the Spirit at all times. We obey the Scripture in all ways. Obeying, always obeying.

Finally, through time and experience—sometimes much time and experience—God begins to give us an amazing settledness in what Thomas Kelly called "the di-

vine Center." In the depths of our being our alternating
gives way to a well-nigh unbroken life of humble adoration
before the living presence of God.

"This is not ecstasy but serenity, unshakableness, firm-
ness of life orientation." In the words of George Fox, we
become "established" men and women. We are developing
a habit of divine orientation. This is not perfectionism but
progress forward in our life with God. The interior work
of prayer becomes much simpler. We experience more enduring upreachings of praise and a relaxed listening in the
depths of our heart. All that is needed to draw us into a
habitual orientation of our heart toward God are little
glances heavenward and quiet whispers of submission.

Without even knowing it we are practicing the presence
of God. Formal times of prayer merely join into and en-
hance the steady undercurrent of quiet worship that un-
derlies our days. Behind the foreground of daily life continues the background of heavenly orientation.

This is the formation of the heart before God. Without
even realizing it our heart is taking on a new character.
Gone are the old impulses for manipulation, anger and re-
venge. Before we are aware of it, in slip new responses of
love and joy and peace and patience and kindness and goodness and faithfulness and gentleness and self-control.

In the words of Thomas Kelly we are entering the experience of "a life of unhurried peace and power. It is simple.

It is serene. It is amazing. It is triumphant. It is radiant. It takes no time, but it occupies all our time. And it makes our life programs new and overcoming. We need not get frantic. He is at the helm. And when our little day is done we lie down quietly in peace, for all is well."

This is the transformation of the human heart, which, in its time and in its way, will lead us irresistibly into "a familiar friendship with Jesus."

Descending with the Mind into the Heart

*The masters of the spiritual life advise that we should,
when contemplating, make use of our imagination. For example,
we should visualize an incident such as the miracle of the
draught of fishes as vividly as we can. We should be present in
mind as though we had just stopped on our way and were
witnessing the event. This is most useful because it brings the
event to life and makes it part of our inner experience.*

ROMANO GUARDINI

*T*HEOPHAN THE RECLUSE, WHOM we met briefly in chapter one, is well recognized in Eastern Orthodoxy, specifically the Russian Orthodox tradition. Theophan was a complex and intriguing personality, but today we know him mostly because of his spiritual writings, especially those on prayer. His homilies on prayer, for example, are a treasure of wise and practical teaching. I mention him here because I have used a phrase from his teaching for the title of this chapter: "To pray is to descend with the mind into the heart, and there to stand before the face of the Lord, ever-present, all seeing, within you."

This statement underscores Theophan's unique ability to break the horns of opposing viewpoints. One group, for example, will insist that prayer is all about the mind, all rational, all cerebral. An opposing group will say, "No, no! Prayer is a matter solely of the heart, of the affections, of intuition." Theophan breaks the horns of this dilemma by taking the key insight of each group and drawing them together in unity—we descend with the mind into the heart.

Meditative prayer does not do violence to our rational faculties. Neither does it confine us solely to the rational. We descend with the mind into the heart. This is a magnificent description of the combination we seek in meditative prayer.

THE SANCTIFIED IMAGINATION

The devotional masters of nearly all persuasions counsel us that we can descend with the mind into the heart most easily through the imagination.* Perhaps some rare individu-

---

*Notable exceptions to this would be the iconoclastic movement of the eighth century, the Quakers of the seventeenth century, the Puritans of the seventeenth and eighteenth centuries and certain fundamentalist groups in our own day.

als can meditate in an imageless void, but most of us need to be more deeply rooted in the senses. We must not despise this simpler, more humble route into God's presence. Jesus himself taught in this manner, making constant appeal to the imagination in his parables, and many of the devotional masters likewise encourage us in this way.

The great Scottish theologian and preacher Alexander Whyte urges us to experience "the divine offices and the splendid services of the Christian imagination." St. Teresa of Avila said, "This was my method of prayer; as I could not make reflection with my understanding, I contrived to picture Christ within me. . . . I did many simple things of this kind. . . . I believe my soul gained very much in this way, because I began to practice prayer without knowing what it was." Many of us can identify with her words, for we too have tried a merely cerebral approach and found it too abstract, too detached. Even more, the imagination helps to anchor our thoughts and focus our attention. Francis de Sales noted that "by means of the imagination we confine our mind within the mystery on which we meditate, that it may not ramble to and fro, just as we shut up a bird in a cage or tie a hawk by his leash so that he may rest on the hand."

Some have objected to using the imagination out of concern that it is untrustworthy and could even be used by the evil one. There is good reason for concern, for the imagination, like all our faculties, has participated in the Fall.

But just as we can believe that God can take our reason (fallen as it is) and sanctify it and use it for his good purposes, so God can sanctify the imagination and use it for his good purposes. Of course, the imagination can be distorted by Satan, but then so can all our faculties. God created us with an imagination, and as Lord of all creation he can and does redeem it and use it for the work of the kingdom of God.

To believe that God can sanctify and utilize the imagination is simply to take seriously the Christian idea of incarnation. God so accommodates, so enfleshes himself into our world that the Lord uses the images we know and understand to teach us about the unseen world of which we know so little and which we find so difficult to understand. Indeed, in one important sense faith is the highest act of the sanctified imagination.

A. W. Tozer penned an essay titled "The Value of the Sanctified Imagination" in which he wrote, "I long to see the imagination released from its prison and given to its proper place among the Sons of the new creation." As we enter more and more into God's way—thinking God's thoughts after him, delighting in the divine presence—we experience God more and more, utilizing our imagination for his good purposes. As we come to truly delight in God, our desires will increasingly please him, which is why they will come to pass (Ps 37:4). In fact, the common experience of those who walk with God is that of being given images of what could be, what should be. So may I encourage you to allow the Lord to give you many delightful images and pictures of God's desire for humanity.

THE IMAGE OF THE INVISIBLE GOD

Since I mentioned the word "pictures," I would like to bring to your attention one physical extension of the imagination that has helped numerous people: namely, the use of icons. The Christian tradition that has developed the most sophisticated and practical understanding of icons has been the Eastern Orthodox Church. The icon in Eastern Orthodox thought is considered a kind of window between the earthly and the spiritual worlds.

This issue was examined in a definitive way in the eighth century through what was called the iconoclastic controversy. The great theologian John of Damascus, in his work *The Fountain of Knowledge*, provided a clear theology for the use of icons in Christian devotion. He taught, in summary, that before God took human form in Christ, no material depiction was possible and therefore blasphemous even to contemplate. Once God became incarnate, however, depiction became possible. Since Christ is God and part of the triune Community, it is justified to hold in our mind the image of God incarnate. Hence, because of the incarnation of Christ, using physical images of Jesus becomes part of a full incarnational, or enfleshment, theology.

The seventh ecumenical council of 787 (the final truly "ecumenical" gathering) settled the matter for the Christian community by affirming the use of icons and other symbols as a valid aspect of Christian worship. In expressing this conclusion, the council was careful to make a clear distinction between the veneration of icons and the worship of icons: supporting their veneration and forbidding their worship. The historian Williston Walker states that veneration of icons can be seen as "an affirmation of the Chalcedonian doctrine of the full and distinct human nature of Christ."

A biblical anchor for this approach is Paul's teaching in Colossians 1:15 that Jesus is "the image (icon) of the invisible God." As we lovingly behold the icon, we seek to pass beyond the image in wood or paint to the person of Jesus himself, and from the person of Jesus into the very presence of the triune God. It is much like when we lovingly touch the photograph of a loved one; we seek to somehow pass beyond the paper to the person himself or herself. Alongside icons candles are often used to symbolize Christ as the light of the world.

Icon painting in the Eastern tradition is not an opportunity for artistic expression as we are accustomed to seeing it in the personalized, creative traditions of the West. Icon paintings are highly stylized and only two-dimensional. All of this is intended to keep us from idolizing the icon and moving past the image into the reality the image represents. The icon is a "window onto heaven," as it is often put.*

READING FOR FORMATION

It is in meditation upon Scripture where we find the "sanctified imagination" used most frequently. Indeed, this way of approaching the sacred text has a long and time-honored history among the people of God. It even has a special name: *lectio divina*, "divine reading" or "spiritual reading."

What does *lectio divina* mean? Well, it means listening to the text of Scripture—really listening, listening yielded and still. It means submitting to the text of Scripture, allowing its message to flow into us rather than attempting to master it. It means reflecting on the text of Scripture, allowing both mind and heart to be fully engaged in the meaning of the passage. It means praying the text of Scripture, letting the biblical reality give rise to our heart cry of gratitude, confession, lament and petition. It means applying the text of Scripture, seeing how God's Holy Word provides a personal word for our life

---

*I write this to you as someone who does not personally use icons. This is not out of theological conviction—that issue was settled at the seventh ecumenical council. It is simply a matter of personal practice—icons have never seemed to speak to my condition. If you want to learn more, I recommend Henri J. M. Nouwen, *Behold the Beauty of the Lord: Praying with Icons* (Notre Dame, Ind.: Ave Maria, 2007).

circumstances. It means obeying the text of Scripture, turning, always turning away from our human ways and into the way everlasting.

Most of all *lectio divina* means seeing the text of Scripture, engaging the sanctified imagination in the full drama of God's Word. St. Francis de Sales counseled, "Represent to your imagination the whole of the mystery on which you desire to meditate as if it really passed in your presence. For example, if you wish to meditate on our Lord on the Cross, imagine that you are on Mount Calvary, and that you there behold and hear all that was done or said on the day of the Passion." Alexander Whyte declared, "With your imagination anointed with holy oil, you . . . open your New Testament. At one time, you are the publican: at another time, you are the prodigal . . . at another time, you are Mary Magdalene: at another time, Peter in the porch . . . till your whole New Testament is all over autobiographic of you."

Lectio divina is a meditative, spiritual reading in which both the mind and the heart are drawn into the love of God. When he was at Harvard, Henri Nouwen once showed me a lovely picture hanging on his apartment wall. The picture depicted a woman holding an open Bible in her lap, but her eyes were lifted upward, as if toward heaven. The idea is that in *lectio* we are both reading the words and attending to the Lord high and lifted up.

We are told that after all the enormous events surrounding Jesus' birth "Mary treasured all these words and pondered them in her heart" (Lk 2:19). In *lectio* we are learning to do the same.

Suppose we want to meditate on Jesus' staggering statement, "My peace I give to you" (Jn 14:27). Of course we will want to study the context of the statement—who said it, when it was said, the teaching surrounding it. We might seek to reconstruct the upper-room scene. We might consider the cost at which our sacrificial Lamb is able to offer us peace. We might even resolve to face a difficult encounter with our employer or with a neighbor in a more peaceful manner.

With *lectio*, however, we do more. We seek to be initiated into the reality of which the passage speaks. We brood on the truth that Jesus is now filling us with his peace. The heart, the mind and the spirit are awakened to his inflowing peace. We sense all motions of fear stilled and overcome by the spirit of "power and of love and of a sound mind" (2 Tim 1:7 KJV). Rather than dissecting peace we are entering into it. We are enveloped, absorbed, gathered into his peace. And the wonderful thing about such an experience is that the self is quite forgotten. We no longer worry about how we can make ourselves more at peace, for we are attending to the infilling of peace into our hearts. No longer do we labor to think up ways to act peacefully, for acts of peace spring spontaneously from deep within.

Perhaps we want to meditate on the story of the feeding of the five thousand (Mt 14:13-21; Mk 6:30-44; Lk 9:10-17). We can see the scene: the multitudes, the hillside, the rocks, most of all the Master himself. We hear the sounds all around us: the chatter of children, the soft breeze blowing across the grasses, a baby crying in her mother's arms, most of all the embracing voice of Jesus himself. We feel the scene: crowds pushing and shoving, hearts eager to hear a word from the Lord, the heat of the day, most of all the calming voice of the Nazarene. We watch as evening comes and sense the hunger among the people but also their reluctance to leave. We watch the whole scene unfold: the discussion about what to do, the five loaves and two fishes, the blessing, the amazement as all five thousand, plus women and children, are fed. We bask in the wonder of it all. The jubilation. We experience everything as if we were truly there.

Finally the multitudes disperse and Jesus walks up into the hills. We are alone. We sit on a rock overlooking the water lapping up on the shore. In our mind we rehearse all that has just transpired. We are quiet. Then Jesus walks up and sits on a rock beside us. Together we are quiet for a time. Then Jesus speaks: "What may I do for you?" And we tell him . . . whatever is in our heart. We receive his healing and blessing. Once again we are still. Finally, we turn and ask the Master, "What may I do for you?" And we listen . . . . this is *lectio*.

Many passages of Scripture can provide a touchstone for meditative prayer: "Abide in my love." "I am the good shepherd." "Rejoice in the Lord always." "For by grace you have been saved through faith." "Be strong in the Lord and in the strength of his power." "I am crucified with Christ." And more. In each case we seek to discover the Lord near to us and long to encounter his presence.

SO GREAT A CLOUD OF WITNESSES

While we always want to affirm the centrality of Scripture, *lectio* includes more than the Bible. We can learn from the lives of the saints and the writings that have proceeded from their profound experience of God. Humbly we read these writings because we know that God has spoken in the past. We read Augustine's *Confessions* and A. W. Tozer's *The Pursuit of God*, Teresa of Avila's *Interior Castle* and Dietrich Bonhoeffer's *The Cost of Discipleship* because we know that they walked with God and we can learn from their experience. It is no accident that the rule of St. Benedict made *lectio* an integral part of daily life. This prayerful reading, as we might call it, edifies us and strengthens us. Whether we are reading about William Wilberforce of England or Sundar Singh of India or Basilea

Schlink of Germany or Ni To-sheng (Watchman Nee) of China, we are encouraged in the life of faith.

So whether through Scripture, icons or the lives of faithful Christians down through the centuries, we are ever seeking to "descend with the mind into the heart, and there to stand before the face of the Lord."

Entering the Experience

Worship at Quaker Meadow

*When I came into the silent assemblies of God's people, I felt
a secret power among them, which touched my heart. And
as I gave way to it, I found the evil in me weakening, and the
good lifted up. Thus it was that I was knit into them and united
with them. And I hungered more and more for the increase of
this power and life until I could feel myself perfectly redeemed.*
Robert Barclay

While experiences of meditation often come to the
individual, they can also be experienced in communal
worship. The power of Christ in a gathered community
can be an awesome thing. A quickening Presence somehow
breaks down the isolation of our individual lives and unites
us together in ways we could never imagine nor create on
our own. This is the story of one such gathering.

I had been asked to be the speaker for a college weekend
gathering in California's high Sierra Mountains. The camp
name was "Quaker Meadow," a place preserving nature's

alpine beauty—rustic by intention and all the more charming because of it.

I had been there before. My conversion ("convincement" is the Quaker term) to the way of Christ and early Christian nurture was in an evangelical Quaker context. My parents came from an eclectic background of Baptist and Church of Christ, but when they both became seriously ill and eventually died, it was the Quakers who surrounded my brothers and me with Christian concern and care. They helped me even more in an unexpected way. When the money I had so carefully tucked away for a hoped-for college education had, little by little, been used up for my mother's medical needs, this Quaker group determined to send me to college. And they did—four years of college and three years of graduate school. As you can imagine, my debt to them was huge.

As a teenager I had gone to Quaker Meadow each July, enjoying the mountain hikes and chapel services and all-over activities of camp. Each day we had a one-hour "discipline of silence," and it was there I learned by experience the prayer of stillness.

Oh, and something else which was not part of the regular camp program. Early each morning I would hike up a little hill overlooking the camp and a small alpine lake. It was dubbed the "Garden of Prayer" and had on one end a rough-hewn cross and on the other a sturdy, hand-built stand with a log book for any who desired to write comments or prayers. In the "garden" itself were a scattering of small boulders half buried in the earth and a covering of pine needles on the ground. Red and white firs surrounded the area. Each morning, bundled in a warm hooded parka, I would seat myself on a cold boulder and make my first stumbling efforts at prayer. I asked for my parents' healing—it wasn't to be. And I memorized 1 Peter 1:7: "That the trial of your faith, being much more precious than of gold that perisheth, though it be tried with fire, might be found unto praise and honour and glory at the appearing of Jesus Christ" (KJV). Quaker Meadow was a special place for a teenager whose parents were dying. One more thing: it was at Quaker Meadow, some forty-plus years ago now, at Inspiration Point that I asked Carolynn to be my bride.

❋   ❋   ❋

So when the request came to speak at Quaker Meadow, I was honored to be sure. Right then I was also in the final throes of graduate doctoral work. The timing could not have been worse. Still . . . in the end I accepted the invitation. I felt enormous pressure—all of my own making— to accept. Even though I knew the feeling was unnecessary, still I felt pressured into speaking.

I kept my feelings to myself and proceeded to prepare for my speaking assignment as best I could. Several months before the retreat itself, the leaders for the gathering met together to make detailed plans. I brought outlines of my talks, determined to show those in charge how seriously I was taking my responsibilities. The leader for the evening observed that often before a planning meeting people would have a perfunctory prayer for guidance. "Instead," he said, "I suggest that we really pray for guidance." So this group, perhaps a dozen in number, entered into a most amazing time of worship. The entire time—perhaps an hour—was pervaded by a living silence. Scriptures were read. Prayers were offered. Songs arose spontaneously. There was a sweet spirit among us, and we knew we were experiencing "the Presence in the midst."

Just then Bill Cathers, a veteran missionary of many years, looked directly at me (perhaps I should say he looked right through me) and asked, "Richard, are you feeling pressured to speak at this retreat?" There it was, the exact feelings I had harbored since accepting the invitation. I had been found out. Bill had seen into my soul. Perhaps more accurately, Bill had been shown the condition of my soul. His question was simple and direct and carried not a hint of condemnation or ridicule. Spoken so gently, it opened up new possibilities for me and for the entire group. In the end I was still to be the appointed speaker, but a fresh openness had seeped into my feelings about the event itself. We ended the planning meeting with a holy expectancy for what God would give us at the retreat.

❈   ❈   ❈

Anytime a hundred and fifty college students gather together there is plenty of excitement. Soon they would be scattered in colleges and universities across the country. But for these few days they had come together for worship and fellowship. This was long before the Internet revolution, so we really were cut off from the outside world. Oh, I guess there was a telephone in the small camp office, but it was used only for emergencies. Gear was quickly tossed into rustic cabins. Greetings were given and old friendships were renewed. Dinner was served.

As evening came on we all headed over to the Quaker Meadow chapel, a building of simple beauty. The entire structure was built of lumber harvested from the campsite. The shake roof was in a steep inverted V shape in order to withstand the heavy snows of winter. The cement floor stair-stepped down to the front, which contained a large floor-to-ceiling arched window that looked out onto a pristine alpine meadow tightly surrounded by redwoods and firs. The benches were rough logs split in half so that one half of the log was for sitting and the other half served as a backrest. Quite comfortable in a hard sort of way! The chapel accommodated approximately one hundred fifty souls, so as we streamed in we filled the room comfortably. From all over we had at last come together. But we were not yet gathered together. That was yet to come.

❋   ❋   ❋

Thomas Kelly notes that for a group to experience the Shekinah of God there needs to be some individuals who are already "gathered deep in the spirit of worship. . . . In them, and from them, begins the work of worship. The spiritual devotion of a few persons . . . is needed to kindle the rest, to help those others who enter the service with tangled, harried, distraught thoughts to be melted and quieted and released and made pliant, ready for the work of God and His Real Presence." Those planning leaders who had gathered a few months earlier were just such individuals. They came with kindled hearts, opening for all of us the gates of worship, adoration, submission and confession.

The leader for our time together was a college professor and a good friend of many years. After giving greetings he shared three words of instruction for our worship. One, that we would "center down." Two, that we would together seek to be "gathered" into the power of God. Three, that we would not run ahead nor lag behind the guiding of the

Holy Spirit, the true Leader of our worship. These three words need a little unpacking.

To center down in a Quaker context means to let go of all distractions and feelings; to become fully present to what is happening here, now; to silence our mind, which is askew with meandering thoughts, and our mouth, which is full of many words.

To be "gathered" means a breaking down of the wall between our separate personalities; a blending of our spirits and hearts together; an experiencing of the language of worship as "we" rather than "me." George Fox counseled, "Mind that which is eternal, which gathers your hearts together up to the Lord, and lets you see that ye are written on one another's heart."

To keep from running ahead or lagging behind the Spirit's leading sounds straightforward enough. But it is an essential counsel if we are to balance our all-too-human tendencies toward the extremes of unbridled enthusiasm or backward reticence. In the seventeenth century William Penn admonished the friends of Jesus, "Therefore brethren, let us be careful neither to run out ahead of our guide, nor loiter behind him; since he that makes haste may miss his way, and he that stays behind may lose his guide."

This is a desperately needed admonition for our contemporary culture. Besides, for us to truly follow such an admonition we need a spiritual attentiveness that is seldom seen today. Nor even asked of us. Robert Barclay wrote, "When assembled, it should be the great task of one and all to wait upon God . . . in order to feel the presence of the Lord in the midst and to know a true gathering in his name according to his promise."

The worship and planning session in preparation for this gathering gave me the freedom to have no predetermination either to speak or to remain silent. Rather, I was to be "baptized into a sense of the meeting," as Quakers sometimes put it.

※ ※ ※

One wonderful gift of a setting such as Quaker Meadow was that time was our friend. No one had some meeting to run off to or a time clock to punch. Hence, what transpired in our worship went on through the evening. I had no watch to check the time, but today, thinking back on our experience, I imagine our worship lasted three or four hours. I was not aware of the time, but I was keenly aware of three distinct movements of the Spirit in our worship experience. I will do my best to describe these movements, but I am very much aware that in these matters words are only fragmentary approximations of the reality. The experience was ineffable and cannot be completely captured in human language.

After an initial period of uninterrupted silence, different ones from various places in the room would break out in a hymn of worship. We would all join in as best we could. I particularly noted that these were not the choruses of personal experience so popular even in that day. Rather, they were stately hymns extolling the wonder-filled goodness of God. God's character. God's mercy. God's faithfulness. And more. I could see that everyone was covered in an immense sense of adoration. I watched this, astonished that college students would be so drawn in and filled with a sense of the Presence in the midst. I too was taken up into a sense of a new Life and Power covering us all. I suppose that this worship-filled singing of hymns extolling the resplendent glory of God went on for perhaps an hour or so.

Then the tenor of the worship experience changed completely. A hush fell over the group as we waited upon the Lord. Then, without human prompting of any kind, different ones would stand and speak words of confession. One after another. At times someone would rise and move over to another person in the room. Together they would speak words of forgiveness and acceptance to one another. Tears flowed. The rest of us sat quietly, reverently as this work of reconciliation went forward. We all sensed an abiding in grace and an overcoming of the spirit and power of darkness. Again, I imagine this process continued on for another hour or so, but I could not tell for time seemed suspended. Robert Barclay explains that in worship there is "an inward travail and wrestling . . . while each is seeking to overcome the evil in themselves." This we felt and this we experienced.

Then a third distinct experience began to flow over the group. Songs of praise and thanksgiving began to erupt spontaneously. We had been caught up into a vaster Life and Power, and deep joy seemed to burst forth among us. This time the songs were completely different from the first part of the worship experience. A group experience of joy and exultation and jubilation pervaded everything. As I watched the group, I considered how inappropriate these songs would have been at the beginning of our worship and how very appropriate they were now. We continued on in this way for another hour or so, and then the glory receded and the meeting was closed.

✳   ✳   ✳

Have other experiences of this nature occurred to me since? Yes, but each time they were original and unlike the former experience. In Jesus we have a living Teacher who comes to us each time in a new and living way. Also, such experiences have been few and far between.

It is not wise for us to hanker after such heights. Worship can be fully valid when there are no thrills or flights of ecstasy. The group, just like the individual, must learn to endure spiritual weather of all kinds with serenity of soul. The heights are full of wonder, but in between those heights we may well travel together through shadow and valley and desert for months and even years. That is all part of what it means to walk with God.

Our prayers, whether individual or corporate, may seldom be filled with ecstasy. No matter. The heart oriented toward God is what is required. Karl Rahner said it well: "Prayer . . . is the raising of the heart and mind to God in constantly renewed acts of love." If we do that, we will have done enough.

PART II

Stepping into Meditative Prayer

He himself is my contemplation;
he is my delight.
Him for his own sake
I seek above me;
from him himself I feed within me.
He is the field in which I labour;
He is the fruit for which I labour.
He is my cause;
He is my effect.
He is my beginning;
he is my end without end.
He is, for me, eternity.

ISAAC OF STELLA

Let the words of my mouth, and the meditation of my heart, be
acceptable in thy sight, O LORD, my strength, and my redeemer.

PSALM 19:14 KJV

Being Present Where We Are

*The price of true recollection is a firm resolve to
take no wilful interest in anything that is not useful
or necessary to our interior life.*

THOMAS MERTON

*I*N BIBLICAL TIMES PEOPLE WERE well versed in how to
meditate; it was in the air they breathed. Today, however,
the situation is quite different. The word itself is not unfa-
miliar, but the language associated with that word is an
ocean away from Christian thinking. It is all about emptying the mind and merging with the cosmic consciousness
and more. To be sure, there is an emptying in Christian
thought, an emptying of all that opposes the way of Christ.
The inside of the cup must be cleaned, as Jesus teaches us
(Mt 23:26). The weight of Christian teaching on meditation, however, focuses on filling both mind and heart with
God, the Creator of all things. Consider the words of Frederick W. Faber:

Only to sit and think of God,
Oh what a joy it is!
To think the thought,
To breathe the name;
Earth has no higher bliss.

The tradition of meditation is long and profound all through the life of the church. But today serious teaching and practice from a Christian perspective is minuscule, if present at all. Hence many are helped immensely by a simple description of the three basic steps into meditative prayer. This chapter will focus on the first step: recollection.

UNDERSTANDING RECOLLECTION

Recollection involves a re-collecting of ourselves until we are unified or whole. The idea is to let go of all competing distractions until we have become truly present where we are. Sometimes anchoring our mind to a brief Scripture phrase or passage helps us in recollection. Evelyn Underhill observed, "In Recollection . . . Christian contemplatives set before their minds one of the names or attributes of God, a fragment of Scripture, an incident of the life of Christ; and allow—indeed encourage—this consideration and the ideas and feelings which flow from it, to occupy the whole mental field."

Let me warn you at the outset: recollection does not come

easily or quickly. Most of us live such fractured and fragmented lives that collectedness is a foreign world to us. The
moment we genuinely try to be collected we become pain-
fully aware of how distracted we really are. Evelyn Underhill notes, "The first quarter of an hour thus spent in at-
tempted meditation will be, indeed, a time of warfare; which
should at least convince you how unruly, how ill-educated is
your attention, how miserably ineffective your will, how far
away you are from the captaincy of your own soul."

One of the genuinely wise teachers on recollection is
Romano Guardini. He is so helpful on this exact point that
it is best to hear his counsel in its entirety:

> Prayer must begin with this collectedness. As said
> before, it is not easy. How little of it we normally
> possess becomes painfully clear as soon as we make
> the first attempt. When we try to compose ourselves,
> unrest redoubles in intensity, not unlike the manner
> in which at night, when we try to sleep, cares or de-
> sires assail us with a force they do not possess during
> the day. When we want to be truly "present" we feel
> how powerful are the voices trying to call us away.
> As soon as we try to be unified and to obtain mastery
> over ourselves, we experience the full impact and
> meaning of distraction. . . . Everything depends on
> this state of collectedness. No effort to obtain it is

ever wasted. And even if the whole duration of our prayer should be applied to this end only, the time thus used would have been well employed. For collectedness itself is prayer. . . . Finally, if at first we achieve no more than the understanding of how much we lack in inner unity, something will have been gained, for in some way we would have made contact with that centre which knows no distraction.

As a beginning experience in recollection we might want to seat ourselves comfortably, and then slowly and deliberately let all tension and anxiety drop away. We become aware of God's presence in the room. If it helps we might picture Christ seated in the chair across from us, for he is truly present. If frustrations or distractions arise, we will want to lift them up into the arms of the Father, letting God care for them. This is not suppressing our inner turmoil but letting go of it. Suppression implies a pressing down, a keeping in check, whereas in recollection we are giving away, releasing. It is even more than a neutral psychological relaxing. It is an active surrendering, a "self-abandonment to divine Providence," to use the phrase of Jean-Pierre de Caussade.

Precisely because the Lord is present with us we can relax and let go of everything, for in the divine Presence nothing really matters, nothing is of importance except attending to God. We allow inner distractions and frustrations to melt away as snow before the sun. We allow God to calm the storms that rage within. We allow God's great silence to still our noisy heart.

A GLAD SURRENDER

Several things occur in the process of recollection. First, there is a glad surrender to him "who is and who was and who is to come, the Almighty" (Rev 1:8). We surrender control over our life and our destiny. In an act of deliberate intention we decide to do things God's way and not our way.

We surrender our possessiveness and invite God to possess us in such a way that we are truly crucified with Christ and yet truly alive through his life (Gal 2:19-20). We relinquish into God's hands our imperialist ambitions to be greater and more admired, to be richer and more powerful, to be saintlier and more influential.

We surrender our cares and worries. "Cast all your anxiety on him, because he cares for you," said Peter (1 Pet 5:7). And so we do, precisely because we sense God's loving care. We are enabled to give up the need to watch out for number one because we have One who is watching out for us.

It may be helpful to picture a box in which we place every worry and every care. When it is full, we gift-wrap it, placing a lovely big bow on top, and give it up as a present to the Father. God receives it, and we must not take it back, for to take back a gift once given is most discourteous.

We surrender our good intentions and high resolves, for even these can harbor the seeds of pride and arrogance. Before she died Mother Teresa of Calcutta said, "Pray for me that I not loosen my grip on the hands of Jesus even under the guise of ministering to the poor." Her words are insightful here, for if we "loosen our grip on the hands of Jesus," we have lost everything. So we surrender all distractions—even good distractions—until we are driven into the Core.

A SPIRIT OF REPENTANCE AND CONFESSION

A second thing that occurs within us as we learn recollection is the rise of a spirit of repentance and confession. Suddenly we become aware—keenly aware—of our shortcomings and many sins. All excuses are stripped away; all self-justifications are silenced. A deep, godly sorrow wells up within for the sins of commission and the sins of omission. Any deed or thought that cannot stand in the searching light of Christ becomes repulsive not only to God but to us as well. Thus humbled under the cross we confess our need and receive his gracious word of forgiveness.

You may wonder if the Lord really needs to hear our confession since God already knows all things. Indeed, but as Søren Kierkegaard observed, "Not God, but you, the maker of the confession, get to know something by your act of confession." And what is it that we get to know? Well, for one thing we learn a little more about our own heart. One reason we cannot program our own heart is because we simply do not understand the depths of the human heart, most especially our own. But as we make confession, God is able then to peel back a few more layers of our heart and give us a glimpse into things we did not know about ourselves. This is all part of the process of heart transformation.

I hasten to add that not only are sin and evil and wickedness revealed in our confession but also goodness and light and life that we never knew about ourselves. Gordon Cosby, the well-known pastor of the Church of the Savior in Washington, D.C., wrote, "Confession has to do with the facing and naming before God the darkness within us; it is also concerned with facing and naming before God the light within as it breaks forth with ever-increasing brilliance. Without a preparatory time of confession no real silence is possible."

To help us in our confession we may want to picture a path littered with many rocks. Some are small pebbles, others are quite large, and still others are almost completely buried so that we cannot know their size. With compunction of heart we invite the Lord to remove each stone, for they do indeed represent the many sins and sorrows littering our lives. One by one our loving Lord picks them up, revealing to us their true character and offensiveness. To our eyes some look big and others small, but the Lord helps us to understand that when lifted the smallest pebble has the same weight as the largest boulder. Some rocks that represent sins committed against us need to be dug out of the ground. While this is painful, it also brings healing. When we see the path completely clear, we rejoice in this gracious work of the Lord.

ACCEPTING THE WAYS OF GOD

A third reality that works its way into our hearts as we experience recollection is an acceptance of the ways of God with human beings. You see, it is one thing to love God; it is quite another to love God's ways. The Bible is clear that God's ways are not our ways, that God's thoughts are not our thoughts (Is 55:8). This passage goes on to explain God's ways:

> For as the rain and the snow come down from heaven,
>   and do not return there until they have watered
>   the earth,
> making it bring forth and sprout,
>   giving seed to the sower and bread to the eater,
> so shall my word be that goes out from my mouth;
>   it shall not return to me empty,

but it shall accomplish that which I purpose,
  and succeed in the thing for which I sent it.
(Is 55:10-11)

God's ways are like the rain and snow that gently fall
and sink into the earth . . . and up comes the life. What a
contrast with our ways, which involve wanting to open up
another person's head and tinker around in there a bit! But,
you see, God's ways are all patience and love, all grace and
mercy. Our ways are all domination and control, all manipulation and guile.

With an inner knowing born out of friendship with Jesus, we begin to see that God's ways are altogether good.
Our impatience, our rebellion, our nonacceptance give
way to a gentle receptiveness to holy impulses. This is not
some stoic resignation to "the will of God." It is an entering
into the rhythm of the Spirit. It is a recognition that God's
commandments are "for our good always" (Deut 6:24). It
is a letting go of our way and a saying yes to God's way, not
grudgingly but because we know it is the better way.

To aid our sense of accepting God's ways, we might
want to imagine ourselves on a lovely beach observing the
footprints of God in the sand. Slowly we begin to place our
feet into the prints. At some places the stride looks far too
long for our small frame; at other places it looks so short
that it appears childlike. In infinite wisdom God is stretch-

ing us where we need to be on the edge of adventure, re-
straining us where we need greater attentiveness and stillness. As we follow God's lead, we enter more and more
into the divine Stride, turning where God turns, accepting
God's ways and finding them altogether good.

Are we present where we are? Sadly, we have to admit
that often we are far removed from where we are. Perhaps
our mind is stewing over a problem at the office when we
should be attentive to our kids. Or we are mentally and
emotionally off on a fishing trip when we should be attending to the people around us. Or when we start to pray, we
are anywhere but in the presence of God. Recollection is
that aspect of meditative prayer that can help draw us more
fully into the place where we are. As this becomes a pattern of life, we will find ourselves more fully alive, more
united and whole.

5

Beholding the Lord

The best contemplative tradition is often inclined to pass on from listening to a tranquil beholding.

HANS URS VON BALTHASAR

As WE EXPERIENTIALLY LEARN the grace of recollection, we begin to move into the second step of meditative prayer, "beholding the Lord." What does this mean? Beholding the Lord speaks of an inward steady gaze of the heart upon God, the divine Center. We bask in the warmth of God's presence. We soak in God's love and care. The soul, ushered into the Holy Place, is transfixed by what she sees.

TWO ANCIENT WITNESSES

Perhaps the best way we can understand this step into meditative prayer is to hear the stories of witnesses of such an experience. One such witness is the fourteenth-century English writer, Bible translator and hermit Richard Rolle of Hampole. What an intriguing person he was! He studied at Oxford, learning Latin there. He also learned about sin there; hence he left Oxford so he could reorder his priorities. He fashioned a rough-and-tumble hermit's habit out of his father's rain hood and two of his sister's tunics. When his sister saw what he had done, she cried, "My brother is mad! My brother is mad!" Later at a local church, after the Mass and with the celebrant's blessing, Rolle mounted the pulpit and preached a sermon "of such sincerity and beauty that 'the multitude could not refrain from tears,' saying 'they had never before heard a sermon of such virtue and power.'"

But now on to his experience of beholding the Lord. Rolle witnessed that as he entered the gaze of the heart upon the Lord, he experienced intense heat around his heart as if it were actually on fire. "It was real warmth too, not imaginary, and it felt as if (my heart) were actually on fire. I was astonished at the way the heat surged up, and how this new sensation brought great and unexpected comfort. I had to keep feeling my breast to make sure there was no physical reason for it!"

Once Rolle was certain there was no material cause for the sensation but that it was purely a gracious gift of God, he added, "I was absolutely delighted and wanted my love to be even greater. And this longing was all the more urgent because of the delightful effect and the interior sweetness which this spiritual flame fed into my soul. Before the infusion of this comfort I had never thought that we exiles could possibly have known such warmth, so sweet was the devotion it kindled. It set my soul aglow as if a real fire was burning there."

Now, I imagine that few if any of us will ever have the physical sensations that Rolle experienced, but we all can seek after the gaze of the heart.

The second witness I bring to you is the seventeenth-century French aristocrat and mother Madame Jeanne Guyon. Guyon's most famous disciple, François Fénelon, spread her teachings far and wide throughout France and beyond. Guyon's superb book *Experiencing the Depths of Jesus Christ** contains helpful teaching for us on the experience of beholding the Lord.

In learning to behold the Lord, Guyon teaches us to use Scripture, but not in the way we learned in *lectio divina*. Here the Scripture is used to quiet the mind. We begin, says Guyon, by reading a passage of Scripture, but as we read, we pause. Guyon explains, "The pause should be quite gentle. You have paused so that you may set your mind on the Spirit. You have set your mind *inwardly*—on Christ." We need to remember, explains Guyon, that we

---

*Written in 1685, this book originally had the rather extended title *Short and Very Easy Method of Prayer; Which All Can Practice with the Greatest Facility, and Arrive in a Short Time, by Its Means, at a High Degree of Perfection*. For writing this book Guyon was put in prison for a little over seven years.

are not reading the Scripture to gain some understanding but to "turn your mind from outward things to the deep parts of your being. You are not there to learn or to read, but . . . to experience the presence of your Lord!"

Once we sense the Lord's presence, the content of what we have been reading has served its purpose. We now hold our heart in God's presence. We do this solely and utterly by faith, says Guyon: "Yes, by faith you can hold your heart in the Lord's presence. Now, waiting before Him, turn all your attention toward your spirit. . . . (The Lord is found *only* within your spirit, in the recesses of your being, in the Holy of Holies; this is where He dwells. The Lord once promised to come and make His home within you. (John 14:23) He promised to there meet those who worship Him and who do His will. The Lord *will* meet you in your spirit.)"

So, here in God's presence we behold the Lord. We are fully aware of God's presence because, as Guyon teaches us, all outward senses have "become very calm and quiet." We are no longer focused on the surface thoughts of the mind; "instead, sweetly and silently, your mind becomes occupied with what you have read and by that touch of His presence."

What? Are we now to go back to the content of what we have read in Scripture? Well, yes and no. It is not that we think about what we have read, explains Guyon; it is that we feed on what we have read. Throughout we are to discipline our mind to be quiet before the Lord. We are to allow our mind to rest.

This concept of feeding but not thinking is a bit beyond my lived experience. But there is more. Guyon's next direction is the most important of all: "In this very peaceful state, *swallow* what you have tasted. . . . In this quiet, peaceful, and simple state, simply take in what is there as nourishment."

CRACKING OPEN THE DOOR

I don't know about you, but all this lofty talk leaves me a little breathless. And overwhelmed. I'm just hoping to make it through this week. Perhaps you feel the same. Often it seems like our meditations never get past our frustration over the unwashed dishes in the sink or the chemistry exam next week. So what do we do?

Well, I do want to encourage us not to despair or to give up. Instead, I would like to suggest three simple—perhaps I should say elementary—ways that can hopefully crack open the door for us onto the experience of beholding the Lord.

The first way is to be still in the presence of the reflected glory of God that we see in creation. This is no infantile pantheism; rather it is a recognition that the created order, even though affected by the Fall, reflects something of the goodness and glory of God. As Paul put it so well, "Ever since the creation of the world [God's] eternal power and divine nature, invisible though they are, have been understood and seen through the things he has made" (Rom 1:20).

One of the reasons we love the creation so much is that it is always doing the will of the Father. Tree and chipmunk, deer and hawk are all busy doing the will of God. Sometimes after a day immersed in the guile and viciousness of human society, I will say to an old hiking friend, "Let's hit the trail and see some of the will of the Father." Elizabeth Barrett Browning declared:

Earth's crammed with Heaven,
And every common bush afire with God;
But only he who sees, takes off his shoes.

Often, especially when I am writing, I will take a break and hike in a nearby canyon. I am accompanied only by my carved redwood walking stick and a water bottle. In the springtime this canyon is filled with the sights and smells of columbine and larkspur, golden banner and Indian paintbrush. In the winter, however, earth tones dominate. Even the ponderosa pine is darker in winter, blending in with the browns of gamble oak and mountain mahogany.

The absence of leaf and flower makes the boulders of the canyon stand out in rugged relief. They are always here, of course, but in the winter they fill the landscape like giant sentinels. I like the rock—hard and durable.

Often I will brush my hand over one of the conglomerate boulders, studded with stones, all cemented together by ancient pressures.

Right after a good snow has fallen I like to hike down into the canyon alone. Likely I will not see another Homo sapien. But I will hear the creek gurgling beneath the ice. In a strange way its perpetual babble calms me. No doubt other sounds will abound: chipmunk and squirrel scratching for food in the underbrush, and in the trees high above the call of hawk and jay, American goldfinch and dark-eyed junco. I'm sure to find a great variety of tracks in the snow; a reminder that I have many more neighbors than I ever see or hear.

But it is the trees that capture my attention the most, and they lead me into complete silence. It's the patience of the trees—stately, quiet, laden with snow. The trees give me a glimpse into the cosmic patience of God. There among the trees I behold the Lord, the Creator of the trees.

A second way of entering the experience of beholding the Lord is by means of worship music. For me music is often the language of beholding. It is helpful if you can find music that metaphorically will take you from the Outer Court through the Inner Court and into the Holy of Holies (see Ex 37–40).

Now, singing and worshiping are not in themselves beholding . . . but they are perhaps an entryway. In beholding the Lord, music functions a little like Guyon's teaching regarding the use of Scripture. As soon as the music brings us to the Mercy Seat, it has served its purpose. At this point we leave the music behind and attend to the Lord. Here we simply and purely behold the Lord.

I don't want to insist on any particular kind or style of music. "Psalms and hymns and spiritual songs, singing and making melody to the Lord with your heart" is the way the apostle Paul described it (Eph 5:19 ESV). And this is sufficient for me.

I guess I do want to add one qualifier. "Loud" and "excited" seldom draw us in. Instead they stir us up and focus on surface emotions. To be sure, there is a time for those experiences; but not here, not in beholding. So I would suggest worship music that draws us inward rather than outward. Beyond that you will, I am sure, find your way to the music that best embodies this experience for you.

A third way. A simple way, really. There are times we enter experiences that go deeper than human words can express. The wise apostle Paul tells us that the Holy Spirit intercedes for us "with sighs too deep for words" (Rom 8:26). And often there are inward yearnings that cannot quite be caught in human language. For some the gift of tongues, or glossolalia, becomes a means through which our spirit may behold the Holy One of Israel. At other times we enter what St. Teresa of Avila called "the prayer of quiet," where all words become superfluous. In silence we behold the Lord. Words are not needed for there to be communion. Most of all we rest in God's "wondrous, terrible, gentle, loving, all-embracing silence."

An Inward Attentiveness

Be silent, and listen to God. Let your heart be in such a
state of preparation that his Spirit may impress upon you such
virtues as will please him. Let all within you listen to him.
This silence of all outward and earthly affection and of human
thoughts within us is essential if we are to hear his voice.
FRANÇOIS FÉNELON

As we experience the unifying grace of recollection and the liberating grace of beholding the Lord, we are ushered into a third step in meditative prayer, the prayer of listening.

The word *step* here might be misleading. It may imply something a little too clear-cut, as if each step could be sharply distinguished from the others. Such, however, is not the case. All these movements or aspects of meditative prayer interrelate and often splash over into one another. It is a living experience we are describing, and like all living experiences it cannot be defined too rigidly. The Lord is the Creator of infinite variety and at times may turn our little steps into one giant leap or teach us to skip or hop or run or even stand still. Always in glad obedience we follow the voice of the true Shepherd.

When we come to the prayer of listening, we put away all obstacles of the heart, all scheming of the mind, all vacillations of the will. There is a hushing of all "outward and earthy affection," as Fénelon reminds us. A graphic phrase from St. John of the Cross, "My house being now all stilled," instructs us in the quieting of all physical and emotional senses. The experiences of recollection and beholding the Lord have done their work. We are now prepared for an inward attentiveness to divine motions. At the center of our being we feel more alive, more active than we ever do when our minds are askew with muchness and manyness. Something deep inside has been awakened and brought to attention. Our spirit is on tiptoe, alert and listening.

On the Mount of Transfiguration the voice of the Lord came out of the bright, overshadowing cloud saying, "This is my Son, the Beloved; with him I am well pleased; *listen to him!*" (Mt 17:5, emphasis added). And so we listen, really listen.

DISCERNING THE LIVING VOICE OF GOD

Now I want to step back for just a moment to consider how we come to discern the living voice of God from, say, our own random thoughts or even the influence of the evil one. I made a passing statement about the voice of God in the very beginning of the book, but now it is time to explore this idea further.*

The first thing that needs to be said in this regard is that no formula will suffice. Five easy steps or ten quick lessons simply are not sufficient to a living relationship. The well-known teaching on the combining and confirming action of Scripture, circumstances and inner promptings as a means for guidance is certainly helpful but incomplete. We need more. We need personal acquaintance. We need, to use the penetrating phrase of Edward John Carnell, "a filial bond."

Jesus made it clear that his sheep can hear and know his voice (Jn 10:11-15). The real question for us is, how? How do we come to discern the living voice of God? The answer is deceptively simple. We learn to discern the voice of God by experience. Sheep (even our pets) learn to recognize the voice of their owner by means of experience. Babies also quickly recognize the voice of their parents. Jesus, through the Holy Spirit, will guide us into all truth. But to receive this guidance and know that it is from the Holy Spirit, we

---

*It is not possible in this small book to go into this matter in detail. For that I would suggest Dallas Willard, *Hearing God* (Downers Grove, Ill.: Inter-Varsity Press, 1999). I consider *Hearing God* (formerly published under the title *In Search of Guidance*) to be among the finest books ever written on divine guidance and certainly the best in recent years. The thoughts in this section draw heavily upon this book.

need a certain acquaintanceship, a certain personal relationship with our "inward Teacher."

We need to explore this matter of acquaintanceship a bit further. Dallas Willard writes, "Certain factors distinguish the voice of God, just as any human voice can be distinguished from another." He goes on to name those factors: the quality of the voice of God, the spirit of the voice of God and the content of the voice of God.

Regarding the first characteristic he notes, "The quality of God's voice is more a matter of *weight* or impact an impression makes on our consciousness. A certain steady and calm force with which communications from God impact our soul, our innermost being, incline us toward assent and even toward compliance." So a sense of divine authority is characteristic of the voice of the Lord. E. Stanley Jones says, "The inner voice of God does not argue, does not try to convince you. It just speaks and it is self-authenticating."

The second aspect is the spirit of the voice of God. This spirit, says Dr. Willard, "is a spirit of exalted peacefulness and confidence, of joy, of sweet reasonableness and of goodwill. It is, in short, the spirit of Jesus." The small epistle of James describes it this way: "The wisdom from above is first pure, then peaceable, gentle, willing to yield, full of mercy and good fruits, without a trace of partiality or hypocrisy" (Jas 3:17).

The third aspect is the content of the voice of God. "The

content of a word that is truly from God will always conform to and be consistent with the truths about God's nature and kingdom that are made clear in the Bible." God will never lead us contrary to what he has said or done in the past. However, we are not here looking at the incidentals or local customs we find in the Bible. Rather we are focusing on the enduring principles of Scripture. This is why it is so important for us to have a good grasp of the entire tenor of Scripture. These three elements then—quality, spirit and content—will help us learn to discern the voice of God.

Of course, the fact that God speaks to us is no guarantee that we will hear correctly. I can tell you by bitter experience that we will get it wrong sometimes. But then this is all part of our training by means of time and experience to distinguish the voice of the true Shepherd.

Now, I know that all of this sounds a bit complicated in analysis. In practice, however, it flows quite naturally. Jesus is here to teach us himself. We will learn if we have humility of heart.

This brings to mind one of the very first things that happens in us as we wait before the Lord: graciously we are given a teachable spirit. I say "graciously" because without a teachable spirit any word from the Lord that comes to guide us into truth could also harden our hearts. Pharaoh, you remember, heard the word of the Lord and it hardened his heart. No doubt we too will resist any and all instruction unless we are docile. But, if we are truly "willing and obedient," the word of the Lord is life and light to us (Is 1:19).

THE WHISPERS OF GOD

What might we expect to hear as we listen? The whispers of God are so sovereignly personal and individualized that I must not pretend to know what God might want to say to you. I would, however, encourage you to be open to two things: the ordinary and the unusual. What do I mean? Let me illustrate.

In the early days of my experiments in listening to the Lord, I sensed a distinct word to call a friend, a chaplain at a local college, and see how he was doing. The word carried with it the marks of gentle authority that I had come to distinguish as the voice of the Lord. I jotted the idea down on a slip of paper and continued my prayer. A little later I called my friend. Now, you need to understand that I was his pastor, so the first thing I said was, "Ron, I'm not calling to ask you to do a single thing! I am just wondering how you are doing."

His response startled me: "Oh! I'm so glad you called . . ." And out came the deep, pressing needs of his heart. What transpired gave me encouragement that I was on the right track with this listening to the Lord. But the word given was so simple, so ordinary. No flashing lights. No earth-shattering command. Just a simple word that brought comfort and healing to my friend.

Ordinary . . . and unusual. George Washington Carver was one of our great scientists, and he often prayed, addressing God as "Mr. Creator." One night he walked out into the woods and prayed, "Mr. Creator, why did you make the universe?" He listened, and this is what he heard: "Little man, that question is too big for you. Try another!" The next night he walked into the woods and prayed, "Mr. Creator, why did you make man [meaning, the human race]?" He listened and he heard this: "Little man, that question is still too big for you. Try another!" The third night he went into the woods and prayed, "Mr. Creator, why did you make the peanut?" This is what he heard: "Little man, that question is just your size. You listen and I will teach you." And you may know that George Washington Carver invented some three hundred ways to use the peanut. Ordinary. Unusual.

Of course we should not be surprised when the whisper of God leads us into simple acts of service and kindnesses. We are led to deliver a bouquet of flowers to an acquaintance who is out of sorts. We feel prompted to shovel the snow off the sidewalk for a handicapped neighbor. We rise quietly in the morning and fix coffee for our spouse. Daily life affords a multitude of such opportunities to serve.

Nor should we be surprised that the whisper of God is

often for us alone and speaks into our deepest need. Do we need peace? God whispers over us divine Peace. Do we need strength? God whispers over us divine Strength. Always the word given carries with it a *zoë* life that is Life indeed!

One of my favorite mentors for listening prayer is Frank Laubach, the great missionary statesman and "apostle of literacy to the silent billion." His books are simply littered with his experiences of listening to the Lord.* Here is one experience from his early days of literacy work when he was alone on the small island of Mindanao in the Philippines. The experience is best quoted in full.

May 24, 1930

This has been a week of wonders. . . . I shall tell you some of the wonders presently. But just at this moment you must hear more of this sacred evening. The day had been rich but strenuous, so I climbed "Signal Hill" back of my house talking and listening to God all the way up, all the way back, all the lovely half hour on the top. And God talked back! I let my tongue go loose and from it there flowed poetry far more beautiful than any I ever composed. It flowed

---

*Laubach wrote nearly one hundred books, fifteen of which are on the topic of prayer. Some of the best known are *Letters by a Modern Mystic, Learning the Vocabulary of God, You Are My Friends, Game with Minutes, Prayer: The Mightiest Force in the World* and *Channels of Spiritual Power.*

without pausing and without ever a failing syllable for a half hour. I listened astonished and full of joy and gratitude. I wanted a dictaphone for I knew that I should not be able to remember it—and now I cannot. "Why," someone may ask, "did God waste his poetry on you alone, when you could not carry it home." You will have to ask God that question. I only know He did and I am happy in the memory.

A PORTABLE SANCTUARY

The goal, of course, is to bring this stance of listening prayer into the course of daily experience. Throughout all life's motions—balancing the checkbook, vacuuming the floor, visiting with neighbors or business associates—there can be an inward attentiveness to the divine Whisper. The great masters of the interior life are overwhelmingly uniform in their witness to this reality. This is represented well in the famous words of Brother Lawrence: "The time of business does not with me differ from the time of prayer; and in the noise and clatter of my kitchen, while several persons are at the same time calling for different things, I possess God in as great tranquillity as if I were upon my knees at the blessed sacrament." We bring the portable sanctuary into daily life.

Entering the Experience

Trek to Cuthbert's Cave

O my divine Master, teach me this mute language
which says so many things.
Jean-Nicholas Grou

I sit on a boulder at the entrance to Cuthbert's cave trying hard to make sense of the events of the last five days.

I think back to the beginning of our odyssey, when our British Airways flight touched down at London's Heathrow airport Monday morning, September 10, 2001. Traveling with me is Glandion Carney, an African American Christian leader from Birmingham, Alabama. Glandion grew up in the San Francisco Bay area during the radical years of Huey Newton, cofounder of the Black Panther Party, and Eldridge Cleaver, author of *Soul on Ice*. "As I was growing up Newton and Cleaver were heroes," Glandion explains, "icons of freedom and belligerence." He tells me that he was three inches taller in those days due to his Afro hairstyle. Today, however, Glandion is bald and quiet-spoken. Still, he retains that edge of social engagement I have always appreciated in him. Together we had come to England bringing a message of life and hope; we had no idea that a hellish message of death and destruction was only hours away.

※ ※ ※

Bright and early Tuesday morning our little group of five travels to a secluded retreat house in North Yorkshire. The nearest population center is the village of Masham. We stop so Glandion can get some "real English chocolate." He buys five Cadbury chocolate bars and is roundly teased by the others for his purchase. St. Mary's Church in the center of Masham was founded in the seventh century, and the present church structure is mainly Norman with fifteenth-century additions. Nearby is the ruins of Jervaulx Abbey. Founded in 1156, Jervaulx was part of the Cistercian order, one of the great renewal movements in history led by Bernard of Clairvaux. It was ravaged and pillaged in the Dissolution of Monasteries during the reign of Henry VIII, and all that remains today are these magnificent ruins perched among the rolling countryside of the Yorkshire Dales. The literature of the area tells me that the abbey has over one hundred eighty species of wildflowers tucked into its walls and crags.

Our destination is up a small lane, narrow enough that I am thankful no other vehicles are coming from the other direction. The five of us tumble out of the car and stretch. The other member of our team meets us at the retreat house. It is a spectacular day, one I have been looking forward to for a long time. For some ten years I had been watching events in Britain and Ireland and wondering if and when the time would be right for a British expression of Renovaré, our renewal effort. With each trip across the pond I had met Christian leaders and developed friendships, all the while waiting for the right time.

Now is that time. We have come to this small retreat house to sign the official papers making Renovaré Britain and Ireland a registered charity in Great Britain. Glandion and I are representing the U.S. expression of Renovaré. Four Brits are to become our founding board and ministry team: James Catford, soon to be our president; Joyce Huggett, a British author of some note; Roy Searle, a leader in the Northumbria Community; and Rob Warner, a Baptist church planter who has developed a creative ministry in Wimbledon.

The retreat house is cozy—just right for our group of six. The old, exterior stonework encompasses the retreat house, a caretaker's apartment and a wooden paddle wheel no longer in use. The hills surrounding the retreat house are a rich green, perfect for grazing sheep, which I am told is the main industry in the area. The hills also render our cell phones completely useless. We can make no contact with the outside world and feel no need to do so. Conversation is warm and energetic. We are starting a new venture for which we have high hopes. We laugh about being just able to scrape together the ten pounds needed to register with the government. Worship is sweet and the planning is visionary. After a leisurely lunch of mutton stew, we spread the documents on the table. Glandion and I watch as the other four sign their names, establishing Renovaré Britain and Ireland. We sing the doxology and offer prayers of thanksgiving.

The next hours are filled with planning and dreaming the future. Dare we hope for a new renewal movement to sweep across the British Isles? We do dare and we plan accordingly. In the late afternoon we take a stretch break, and several of us determine to climb the largest hill in the region. Once on top James decides to see if his cell phone might have a signal.

❋   ❋   ❋

There on top of a hill in a verdant valley of North Yorkshire we hear the first bewildering word of what has happened half a world away. It is beyond our comprehension and stands in stark contrast to the quiet, pastoral setting all around us.

The couple who care for the retreat house are gracious and invite us to crowd into their small apartment, and together we watch in silence the images of desperate men and women in business garb jump to certain death. Over and over the television plays the footage of commercial airliners slamming into the World Trade Center. Wanton devastation. Absolute horror. Utter shock. We stand there . . . still, dumbfounded.

While we are still trying to wrap our minds around what has happened, the BBC broadcasts the words of Prime Minister Tony Blair: "There have been most terrible, shocking events taking place in the United States of America within the last hour or so including two highjacked planes being flown deliberately into the World Trade Center. I'm afraid we can only imagine the terror and carnage there and the many, many innocent people that will have lost their lives. I know that you would join me in sending the deepest condolences to President Bush and to the American people on behalf of the British people at these terrible events. This mass terrorism is the new evil in our world today. It is perpetrated by fanatics who are utterly indifferent to the sanctity of human life and we, the democracies of the world, are going to have to come together to fight it together and to eradicate this evil completely from our world."

Soon we hear the special notice issued by the FAA

grounding all U.S. flight operations: "Effective immediately until further notice flight operations in the national airspace system by United States civil aircraft and foreign civil and military aircraft are prohibited except for medical emergency, U.S. military, law enforcement and emergency evacuation flights."

What does it all mean? And what has become of United Airlines flight 93, which disappeared from radar somewhere in Pennsylvania? Confusion and questions abound. For us one thing is certain: Glandion and I will not be returning to the U.S. anytime soon.

We continue with our planning for another day and a half, but the tragic events in New York City and Washington, D.C., are never far from our minds.

※　※　※

Rather than return to London, Glandion and I decide to take a train north to Northumberland, specifically the small island of Lindisfarne. In the early days of Celtic Christian mission penetration into the Anglo-Saxon kingdoms, Lindisfarne served as the nerve center. In fact, the stories of mission exploits emanating from here so impressed the popular imagination that eventually Lindisfarne began to take on another name, "Holy Island," and so it is called to this day.

Holy Island is forever linked to the names of St. Aidan and St. Cuthbert. Aidan was the first great missionary leader, coming from Iona on the west coast of Scotland and establishing Lindisfarne on the east coast of England as his base. The most dramatic feature of the island today is the large statue of Aidan holding in his outstretched hand the torch of the gospel while a Celtic cross stands like a wreath behind his head. Cuthbert eventually followed in Aidan's footsteps and, having grown up in the region, he in some ways made an even more dramatic impact than Aidan. I stand on a rocky promontory on Holy Island and nearby I can see a much smaller island known as St. Cuthbert's Island. When the tide is low a land bridge connects Holy Island to Cuthbert's Island and this was where Cuthbert would retreat to when he was seeking complete solitude.

On earlier trips I had gotten to know the Northumbria Community, a vigorous expression of Christian faithfulness in Northumberland that has arisen in recent years.[*] I always feel at home and refreshed anytime I can be with this unique group. The Northumbria Community is a gathering of folk from eclectic backgrounds: Catholic, Anglican, Baptist, unchurched and others. They consciously

---

[*]The Northumbria Community has compiled a prayer book, *Celtic Daily Prayer,* which forms the basis of their community life. I wrote an introduction to the American edition (San Francisco: HarperSanFrancisco, 2002), which contains an early version of the story of my trek to Cuthbert's cave.

seek to embody "the ancient paths" of Christian faithfulness that seem to be etched into every stone and rise out of
the soil of the Cheviot Hills of Northumberland. They attempt to find a practical modern expression of a new mo-
nasticism rooted in the vows of "availability and vulnera-
bility" and hold an uncompromising allegiance to the
imperatives of the Sermon on the Mount.

The Northumbria Community is, by intention, a geo-
graphically dispersed community. However, the nerve
center is close by at Hetton Hall, a sprawling house with a
stone-enclosed prayer garden, two tiny "Poustinias" for
private prayer, and the community chapel. Hetton Hall is
where Glandion and I stay for the next few days as we wait
for international travel to resume. I relish especially the
large kitchen area with its weathered wooden dining table
that could probably seat two dozen if need be. There is always work to do at Hetton Hall . . . and ample opportunity
for conversation and prayer.

※   ※   ※

Nestled high up in the Kyloe Hills above Hetton Hall is
Cuthbert's cave. I had read the stories surrounding this
cave but had never seen it for myself. Even as I write these
words I have in front of me a small watercolor of Cuthbert's cave that reminds me of my sojourn there. The
painting was given to me by one of the companions of the

community, Brenda Grace. It is Brenda who volunteers to take me to see the cave. I drag Glandion along even though he complains that a long hike for him means going from his car to Starbucks for coffee.

In 651 the shepherd boy Cuthbert used this cave as a shelter for the night as he watched over his sheep. One night he saw a stream of light piercing the darkness and choirs of the heavenly host coming down to earth and taking with them a soul of great brightness. The next morning Cuthbert learned that Aidan, bishop at Lindisfarne, had died at the exact hour he had his astonishing vision. Immediately Cuthbert left his shepherd duties and set out for the monastery at Melrose where he offered himself for training for Christian ministry. He would eventually take the place of Aidan and further the Christian cause immeasurably.

Brenda drives us up into the Kyloe Hills until the road ends. We park the car and follow a trail that winds through lush grasses and verdant pines. I let Glandion and Brenda walk a little ahead; right now I long for the quiet of the forest.

At the cave Brenda is eager to take us farther, up atop the rocky promontory that overlooks Holy Island and, in the distance, the Farne Islands, all made famous by Celtic exploits. Once we reach the top, the North Sea wind tugs hard at us, and I can tell that Brenda is eager to return to Hetton Hall. Glandion would like to stay longer, but without Brenda's car the walk back will be a considerable distance. I resolve his dilemma by explaining that I am planning to hike for some time along the trails on the ridge and will be staying at the cave late. Immediately Glandion decides to return with Brenda, a decision I welcome, for right now I crave solitude.

They leave and I do indeed hike along the ridge overlooking the North Sea. The ridge is literally packed with heather for as far as the eye can see. I have heard stories about "the heather on the hills," but nothing prepares me for the sheer beauty of its purple splendor. Time after time I feel obliged to stop and kneel just to gaze at the exquisite bell-shaped flower that the heather produces. There are multiplied millions of these flowers and their very mass overwhelms me, so looking closely at one plant or even a single tiny bloom helps me to absorb its loveliness.

Finally I arrive at the cave itself. I am completely alone; no tourists or visitors disturb my time here. At first I explore the physical aspects of the cave: the gray granite with mosses clinging, the lush ferns and rose-tinted flowers along its edges, the simple handmade cross resting in a crevice in the rock. There is graffiti in the cave, howbeit proper British graffiti—mostly dates neatly carved into the rock. The older dates are too worn for me to read, but I jot down some of the more recent dates—recent, that is, by the standards of British history . . . 1818 David Doucle . . . 1819 W. H. W. . . . 1849 . . . 1861 . . . 1890.

However, I've not come here to explore a cave but to pray. I have brought enough backpacking equipment to stay the night; however, earlier in the day I learned about a gathering of several community companions this evening and the assumption is that I will be joining the group. So my time here is, of necessity, shorter than I had hoped. Still, ample time and space are mine to enter into the prayer of Dag Hammarskjöld:

Give me a pure heart—that I may see Thee,
A humble heart—that I may hear Thee,
A heart of love—that I may serve Thee,
A heart of faith—that I may abide in Thee.

Hammarskjöld's prayer leads me into my own experience of meditative prayer.

It has been four days since the horrific events of September 11 when towers and fortress fell. My mind replays over and over the unbearable images of commercial airliners transformed into missiles of devastation and of the Twin Towers first ablaze and then collapsing, entombing thousands.

At this pivotal point in American history I am away . . . away on a distant shore, away from homeland, away from family and friends and fellow citizens. And yet while away I am also there . . . there in Manhattan and D.C. I too feel pain and anguish and utter disbelief.

The juxtaposition of the horror scenes playing in my

mind's eye and the quiet serenity of Cuthbert's cave is sur-
real. I consider how blatant evil, once unleashed, will by its
very nature produce more evil. Terrible as the scenes of
the last days have been, they may well be only the beginning. Unrestrained evil seems so powerful, so overwhelming right now. What can I . . . what can anyone . . . pray at
a time like this? Only the timeless cry of the heart: *Kyrie
eleison*; Lord have mercy.

This pastoral scene, this quiet cave, seems far removed
from the terror of twisted, burning steel; of families suddenly ripped apart; of fathers and mothers never returning
home; of anguished cries and disbelieving stares. Then I
remember that long ago during the Viking reign of terror
it was to this very cave that many fled, carrying with them
Cuthbert's body in the hope of preserving it from desecra-
tion. Suddenly, without warning, whole villages were
razed, men slaughtered, women raped, children taken into
slavery. This place too has known the horrors of raw evil.
Truly, there is "no hidin' place down here."

Then, right in the midst of my musings, I hear a sound
of hope, a sound so unexpected that it startles me. It is the
song of a meadowlark. Did I really hear it? This is not the
time of year nor the place I would expect to hear a meadowlark. But there it is again, the unmistakable clear, whis-
tling song. So simple, so clear, so strong. It sings to me of
beauty, of hope, of a future beyond all evil and devastation.

Perhaps it is, and by faith I take it to be, a word of encouragement from the loving heart of God. And so the song of the meadowlark frees me to begin praying that the ocean of darkness that seems to engulf us today will, in God's time and in God's way, be overcome by the far greater ocean of God's light and life.

May it be so. Amen.

PART III

Dealing with Everyday Difficulties

Be still, my soul! the Lord is on thy side;
Bear patiently the cross of grief or pain;
Leave to thy God to order and provide;
In every change He faithful will remain.
Be still, my soul! thy best, thy heavenly Friend
Through thorny ways leads to a joyful end.

KATHARINA VON SCLEGEL

O how I love thy law! It is my meditation all the day.

PSALM 119:97 KJV

7

Wandering Minds

At this very moment your thoughts are buzzing like a swarm of bees. The reduction of this fevered complex to a unity appears to be a task beyond all human power. Yet the situation is not as hopeless for you as it seems. All this is only happening upon the periphery of the mind, where it touches and reacts to the world of appearance. At the centre there is a stillness which even you are not able to break.

EVELYN UNDERHILL

*I*N 1994 SVEN BIRKERTS WROTE *The Gutenberg Elegies*, in which he predicted that in a decade or so the electronic revolution would have changed our world beyond recognition: "We will be swimming in impulses and data—the microchip will make us offers that will be very hard to refuse."

Today, we know just how accurate his prediction has become. We click through an endless stream of Internet links, multitask in numerous media, write a daily blog, check our e-mail every few hours, text friends and others regularly throughout the day. Neuroscience studies are now showing that the neural pathways of our brains are being rewired accordingly so that our capacity for sustained attention is decreasing.

Of course, everywhere we go we hear people complaining about our wired world—about how complicated it has made life and about how frustrating it is—all the while utilizing every technological gadget at their disposal. The truth of the matter is we enjoy our technological gluttony. It is all so stimulating and interesting.

Actually, the Internet culture is only a surface issue. Our problem is something far more fundamental. This deeper, more basic issue can be summed up in one word: distraction. Distraction is the primary spiritual problem in our day. The Internet, of course, did not cause this problem; people were distracted long before it came along. Blaise Pascal observed, "The sole cause of man's unhappiness is that he does not know how to stay quietly in his room." The fact that our schedules are piled high and we are constantly bombarded by multiple stimuli only betrays that we have succumbed to the modern mania that keeps us perpetually distracted. The moment we seek to enter the creative silences of meditative prayer, every demand screams for our attention. We have noisy hearts.

Sadly, our Christian worship services are of no help here. Today, for the most part, they have become one huge production in distraction. Worship meant to draw us into the presence of God has become little more than an organized way of keeping us from the presence of God. So it is little wonder that when we are first learning meditative prayer, we need help in how to control a wandering mind.

SMALL BEGINNINGS

The first counsel I would give regarding a wandering mind is for us to be easy on ourselves. We did not develop a noisy heart overnight, and it will take time and patience for us to learn a single-hearted concentration. Dietrich Bonhoeffer offers wise counsel precisely on this point: "The first thing to remember is not to get impatient with yourself. Do not cramp yourself in despair at the wandering of your thoughts. Just sit down each day and wait patiently. If your thoughts keep running away, do not attempt to restrict them. It is no bother to let them run on to their destination; then, however, take up the place or the person to whom they have strayed into your prayers. In this way you will find yourself back at the text, and the minutes of such digressions will not be wasted and will not trouble you."

The inner chatter we experience the moment we try to be still and listen to the Lord no doubt tells us something about our own distractedness. It is not wrong for us to devote the whole duration of our meditation to learning about our own inner chaos. Beyond this, sometimes we need to gently but firmly speak the word of peace to our racing mind and so instruct it into a more disciplined way. Often I will keep a things-to-do pad handy and simply jot down the tasks that are vying for my attention until they have all surfaced. Then the buzzing thoughts can settle down, and I can be still.

If one particular matter seems to be repeatedly intruding into our meditation, we may want to ask of the Lord if the intrusion has something to teach us. That is, we befriend the intruder by making it the object of our meditation.

Now, if we are to deal substantially with the problem of a wandering mind, we need to begin before the actual time of meditation. It is important to find ways in our contemporary circumstances to crucify the spirit of distraction. A beginning way might be to practice a Sabbath time from all electronic media. I would suggest a fast from all our Internet gadgetry for one hour a day, one day a week, one week a year. See if that helps to calm the internal distraction. I have a friend who when leading retreats asks the retreatants to turn in (not just turn off) their cell phones and Black-Berries and iPads. She reports to me that when she makes this request, people look at her as if she had just asked them to cut off their right arm.

WORDS DANCING WITH BEAUTY

I want to offer a counsel for focusing a wandering mind

that may seem strange to you at first. I am talking about the selective reading of poetry. Three things make poetry especially helpful in settling our mind.

First, poetry startles us with its economy of words and beauty of language. This is unusual in our wordy world where advertisers and politicians are constantly prostituting words for sales or votes. Words, carefully chosen and beautifully written, have a way of slowing us down and focusing our attention on essential matters.

Second, if you are anything like me, you simply do not understand what the poet is saying on the first read. This forces us to stop and go back and read the words again. And again. If we are patient, our racing mind slowly will become present to the poem. A poem most often has a double meaning, and it takes us a little while to move past the surface subject of the poem to the deeper issue the poet is after. As we begin to understand the poem, we realize that the racing of our mind has calmed down considerably.

Third, the mind is often captured by the metaphor of a poem. A metaphor, of course, takes two very different things and shows one way in which they are similar. We are employing a metaphor when we call that small, gray computer device we use every day a "mouse." Or think of Robert Frost comparing our life to a journey: "Two roads diverged in a wood, and I—I took the one less traveled by. And that has made all the difference." Our mind is captured by the image of the fork in the road, and that focuses our attention as we think about the choices we have to make in life. So the metaphor in the poem helps to center a wandering mind.

Briefly, I would like to recommend to you three poets: John Donne, George Herbert and a contemporary poet, Robert Siegel. Of course, you may have a favorite poet of your own, or perhaps you enjoy writing poetry yourself.

John Donne is perhaps the greatest of the metaphysical poets of the seventeenth century. We know him, of course, from the famous line, "No man is an island, entire of itself. . . . Therefore never send to know for whom the bell tolls; It tolls for thee." I like him especially for his vivid imagery and overwhelming emotion. Consider this fragment from his *Holy Sonnets*:

> Batter my heart, three-personed God; for you
> As yet but knock, breathe, shine, and seek to mend;
> That I may rise and stand, o'erthrow me; and bend
> Your force to break, blow, burn, and make me new.

George Herbert, of course, was a contemporary of Donne.[*] He wrote an excellent book on spiritual formation in the context of a pastoral setting, *The Country Parson*. But smack in the midst of all the ordinariness of his parish

---

[*]John Donne, 1573-1631; George Herbert, 1593-1633.

life—births and deaths, broken marriages and anxious parents, pastoral visits by the score and cups of tea beyond numbering—Herbert was also writing the most astonishing poetry. And something in his poetry has a way of settling our minds and hearts. You can get the idea quickly from a brief selection from his huge collection of poems called *The Temple*:

If as a Flower doth spread and die,
Thou wouldst extend me to some good,
Before I were by frost's extremity
Nipt in the bud.

Robert Siegel is a wonderful present-day poet. He is already being compared to Keats and others. I am not qualified to comment on such matters, but I am deeply drawn to his uncanny ability to see in the natural world small epiphanies of ordinary life. He writes on all manner of topics, but when he turns to the created order, something mysterious, almost mystical, occurs. Consider this poem which provides the title to his newest book:

Yellow flames flutter
about the feeder:
A Pentecost of finches

Some have called poetry the language of God. I can see why.

A SIMPLE MEDITATION TO FOCUS THE MIND

It feels almost sacrilegious to transition from words that have been cut and chiseled and polished to something as prosaic as a meditation experience. Nonetheless, I want to provide you with a simple handle for dealing with a wandering mind. I call this meditation experience, for lack of a better name, "pull the plugs."*

Find a comfortable setting that is free of distractions. Perhaps a favorite sitting chair. In your imagination you may want to picture Jesus in the chair across from you. He smiles and nods.

Begin by reading or rehearsing in your mind a favorite biblical passage, perhaps the Lord's Prayer or the Twenty-Third Psalm. There are plugs on all ten fingers and all ten toes, and when you are ready, pull these plugs and watch as a cloudy liquid flows out and into a drain in the center of the floor. The liquid represents all the distractions and concerns that occupy your mind. The regrets of yesterday, the responsibilities of today, the fears of tomorrow. As the liquid flows out, you watch as the level drops down, down, down until it is all gone. You then replace the plugs, and Jesus, smiling, comes over, opens the top of your head and begins to fill you with a bright, crystal-clear liquid. This

---

*In *Celebration of Discipline* I describe another meditation experience with a similar purpose called simply "palms down, palms up" (p. 30). You, of course, are welcome to create your own meditation experience.

represents the Word of God, which is filling you to such an extent that there is no room anywhere in you for distraction of any kind. Your body is full of the Word of God. Your mind is full of the Word of God. Your heart is full of the Word of God. All distractions are gone, and in this posture you listen for the Word of the Lord.

François Fénelon wrote, "God does not cease speaking, but the noise of the creatures without, and of our passion within, deafens us, and stops our hearing. We must silence every creature, we must silence ourselves, to hear in the deep hush of the whole soul, the ineffable voice of the spouse. We must bend the ear, because it is a gentle and delicate voice, only heard by those who no longer hear anything else." Oh, may you, may I, hear nothing else.

Like a Roaring Lion

*There are two equal and opposite errors into which our race
can fall about the devils. One is to disbelieve in their existence.
The other is to believe, and to feel excessive and unhealthy
interest in them. They themselves are equally pleased by both
errors, and hail a materialist or a magician with the
same delight.*

C. S. LEWIS

REALITIES RESIDE IN OUR UNIVERSE that go far beyond
what we can see and touch and smell. There are immense
spiritual realities. God, of course. And angels, God's mes-
sengers. The Bible is actually a book full of angels. Please,
I do not mean fluffy white beings with flowing robes and
feathered wings. Nor do I mean the childlike nudes of Ra-
phael or, even worse, the chubby cherubs of today's clip
art. No, in the Bible when an angel appears on the scene,
the angel first must calm the utter panic in humans. When
the angel Gabriel appeared to Zechariah, we are told that

Zechariah "was terrified; and fear overwhelmed him" (Lk 1:12). Also, the angel population evidently is enormous, for we are told in Revelation that surrounding God's throne are angels who number "myriads of myriads and thousands of thousands" (Rev 5:11).

Angels then are spiritual beings of considerable power of an order higher than human beings, but, like humans, they are endowed with free will and not immune to temptation and sin. Hence, Satan and his devils appear on the scene. They are angels—Satan being the chief—who by the abuse of their free will fell and became the enemies of God. And of us. Satan is called many things in the Bible: the devil, Beelzebub, the ruler of this world, the prince of the power of the air, and more (Mt 10:25; Jn 14:30; Eph 2:2).

I have used one of the biblical descriptions of Satan for the title of this chapter. Peter provides the description: "Like a roaring lion your adversary the devil prowls around, looking for someone to devour" (1 Pet 5:8). So the diabolical wickedness of Satan and his minions is clearly something for us to reckon with.

But we must remember that Satan is not co-equal with God. Satan is a created being, a fallen angel. He does not have ultimate power. He is limited in knowledge. C. S. Lewis put it well: "Satan, the leader or dictator of devils, is the opposite, not of God, but of Michael."

True, Satan is "a roaring lion," but I want to remind you

that there is another Lion who is greater than Satan: Jesus, "the Lion of the tribe of Judah, the Root of David" (Rev 5:5). This is the Lion who has conquered sin and death and hell. John declares, "The Son of God was revealed for this purpose, to destroy the works of the devil" (1 Jn 3:8). And again, "The one who is in you is greater than the one who is in the world" (1 Jn 4:4). James tersely admonishes us, "Resist the devil, and he will flee from you" (Jas 4:7).

I say all of this so you may be aware of Satan and his diabolical works of destruction, but also so you will not have an excessive fear of him or of his works. This awareness is important as we deepen in our understanding and experience of prayer. Satan and his minions do seek our destruction, and they will attack us even in times of prayer . . . perhaps especially in times of prayer. So whatever we can learn about Satan and his devious ways will fortify us against being tricked or fooled or drawn astray.

LEARNING FROM JESUS

Jesus is the Master Teacher of life, and his experiential knowledge of Satan and his tactics can instruct us in multiple ways. The most central passage has to be Jesus' forty days in the wilderness. In that single event we see a lifetime of the practiced ability to overcome evil.

We notice at the outset that it is the Spirit, not Satan, who leads Jesus into the wilderness. The Spirit is in charge of all that occurs. Jesus fasts for forty days and only then is Satan allowed to come to him. The fasting was for the spiritual strengthening of the Master, and the Spirit does not allow Satan near Jesus until he is at his strongest point.

God allows the evil one to come at Jesus with three great temptations—temptations that Jesus undoubtedly had dealt with more than once in the carpentry shop and that he would face again throughout his ministry as a rabbi. Yet these are not just personal temptations; they are also temptations for Jesus to access for his own use the three most prominent social institutions of the day—economic, religious, political.*

The economic temptation is for Jesus to turn stones into bread—for Jesus, the glorious miracle baker, to provide "wonder bread" for himself and the masses. What a temptation in a hungry world! But Jesus knows how short-lived all such solutions are and so rejects the live-by-bread-alone option.

The religious temptation is for Jesus to leap from the pinnacle of the temple and, by having angels catch him midair, receive God's stamp of approval on his ministry. God's dramatic rescue within the sacred boundaries of the

---

*For an elaboration of this line of thinking, see Donald B. Kraybill, *The Upside-Down Kingdom* (Scottdale, Penn.: Herald, 1978). See also Richard J. Foster, *Streams of Living Water* (San Francisco: HarperSanFrancisco, 1998) pp. 1-22.

temple will surely guarantee the loyal support of the priestly hierarchy. On this occasion Satan even buttresses his appeal by quoting from Scripture. But Jesus sees Satan's temptation for what it is, and he directly confronts institutionalized religion—not only here in the wilderness but throughout his ministry—wherever and whenever it becomes idolatrous or oppressive.

Satan's ultimate goal is revealed in his third temptation, the promise of "all the kingdoms of the world and their splendor" if only Jesus will fall down and worship him (Mt 4:8-10). This mountaintop temptation represents the possibility of worldwide political power—not only coercive force but also the glory and acclaim of sitting on the world's highest pinnacle of influence and status. Satan knows this fits in perfectly with the messianic hopes of the day for a Savior who will cast off the oppressive Roman occupation. But Jesus knows that domination and force are not God's way. He rejects coercive power because he intends to demonstrate a new kind of power, a new way of ruling. Serving, suffering, dying—these are Jesus' messianic forms of power. Hence, Jesus stoutly resists: "Away with you, Satan! for it is written, 'Worship the Lord your God, and serve only him'" (Mt 4:10).

In those forty days in the wilderness, Jesus rejects the popular Jewish hope for a Messiah who will feed the poor, bask in miraculous heavenly approval and shuck off oppressive nations. In doing so he undercuts the leverage of the three great social institutions of his day . . . and of ours— exploitive economics, manipulative religion and coercive politics. We too must learn to defeat Satan precisely in these realms.

There is more. The Gospels tell multiple stories of how Jesus confronts evil in every form, not only casting out demons but healing sicknesses of all kinds and applying gospel medicine to darkened minds. "Jesus went throughout Galilee . . . proclaiming the good news of the kingdom and curing every disease and every sickness among the people. So his fame spread throughout all Syria, and they brought to him all the sick, those who were afflicted with various diseases and pains, demoniacs, epileptics, and paralytics, and he cured them" (Mt 4:23-24). The apostle Paul's word certainly rings true that in Jesus God "has rescued us from the power of darkness and transferred us into the kingdom of his beloved Son, in whom we have redemption, the forgiveness of sins" (Col 1:13).

In chapter ten of Luke we see a pinnacle insight regarding the defeat of satanic power. Jesus had first sent out the twelve and then the seventy instructing them to "cure the sick . . . and say to them, 'The kingdom of God has come near to you'" (Lk 10:9). They return ecstatic, saying, "Lord, in your name even the demons submit to us!" (Lk 10:17). Now, assured that the power to overcome demonic wickedness is transferable to ordinary disciples, Jesus exclaims, "I saw Satan fall like lightning from heaven" (Lk 10:18 RSV).

Jesus is here seeing the crushing of satanic powers. It is also a prophetic vision of that ultimate day when the one who is called Faithful and True, astride a white battle stallion, will go forth conquering, and to conquer, and "on his robe and on his thigh he has a name inscribed, 'King of kings and Lord of lords'" (Rev 19:11-16). On that day of ultimate and final victory, Satan and all his minions will be cared for once and for all: "And the devil . . . was thrown into the lake of fire and sulfur" (Rev 20:10).

PRACTICAL CONSIDERATIONS

Now, I want us to turn our attention to several practical concerns regarding demonic forces and the life of prayer. First, we are all aware of the great interest today in a whole host of occult practices: witchcraft, astrology, the seeking out of spirit guides, palmistry, tarot readings, Ouija boards and divination of all sorts. Now, I hate to be so blunt on this matter, but these practices are forbidden for the follower of Christ. Demonic spiritual forces can influence and even inhabit such practices.

The early Israelite community faced many of these same practices in the nations around them, and God was quite direct on the matter: "No one shall be found among you who makes a son or daughter pass through fire, or who practices divination, or is a soothsayer, or an augur, or a sorcerer, or one who casts spells, or who consults ghosts or spirits, or who seeks oracles from the dead" (Deut 18:10-11). You may remember the time King Saul consulted the medium at Endor. He encountered spiritual realities there that he was not prepared for, and the end of the matter was not good, to say the least (1 Sam 28).

Second, in prayers for the demonized I would counsel great caution. These settings are often crowded with people who fancy themselves "exorcists" and who will brashly rush into the holy of holies of another person's soul. Such people are often intoxicated with spiritual phenomena and usually lack any real compassion for the person being prayed for. If we are moved by genuine compassion, we will tread lightly and listen prayerfully. If a person is concerned about demonic influence or fearful of it, we may then speak a simple prayer of faith in the love of Jesus and dismiss this troubling spirit, whether real or imagined, giving it into the hands of Jesus. Then we pray for the light and love of Jesus Christ to fill up all the empty spaces in the person.[*]

Third, we should not give Satan too much credit. I have

---

[*]If you would like to pursue these matters further, I suggest you turn to Agnes Sanford, *The Healing Gifts of the Spirit* (New York: J. B. Lippincott, 1966), and John Wimber, *Power Healing* (San Francisco: Harper & Row, 1987).

found that we do a fairly good job of beating up on ourselves without any help from Satan. Once a dear woman, beset by uncontrollable fears and traumas and evil spiritual influences, came to a good friend of mine, one well-trained in compassionate ministry for the demonized. He listened silently to the bizarre story of this tortured woman. At last he placed his hands on her head in the sacramental way and prayed quietly for her. No shouts or stern commands, just compassion-filled prayer ministry. The woman sighed and became calm . . . and healing entered her soul. Later my friend explained simply, "Oh, she had a great big hurt and a little tiny demon."

Fourth, I commend to you prayers of protection for all we do and whenever we pray. Spiritual realities abound in this created order of ours, and they are not all benevolent. Satan and his minions seek our downfall and destruction. So we ask the Holy Trinity and all the heavenly host to surround us and keep us from all ill: physical, spiritual, emotional. Here is a prayer of protection I like very much which comes out of the Celtic tradition of Lindisfarne in the northeast of England:

> Circle me, Lord,
> keep protection near
> and danger afar.
>
> Circle me, Lord,

keep light near
and darkness afar.

Circle me, Lord,
keep peace within;
keep evil out.

In the name of the Father,
and of the Son,
and of the Holy Spirit. Amen.

Frequently I will pray for protection in a highly Christo-centric manner:

O Lord, I pray that you would . . .
Surround me with the light of Jesus Christ;
Cover me with the blood of Jesus Christ; and
Seal me with the cross of Jesus Christ.
This I pray in the name of Jesus Christ.
Amen.

In all of this we need never fear. The almighty God—Father, Son and Holy Spirit—will surround us and protect us and keep us from every evil influence. We can count on it.

A FINAL WORD

I would like to close this chapter by returning to the passage in the first epistle of Peter that is the source of the phrase "like a roaring lion." Peter certainly minces no words about the wiles of the devil and the reality of human suffering. But the overriding message of this passage is fixed firmly upon the great reality of God's sovereign power over all. This is the message that needs to root itself deeply into our hearts and minds. Listen:

> Humble yourselves therefore under the mighty hand of God, so that he may exalt you in due time. Cast all your anxiety on him, because he cares for you. Discipline yourselves, keep alert. Like a roaring lion your adversary the devil prowls around, looking for someone to devour. Resist him, steadfast in your faith, for you know that your brothers and sisters in all the world are undergoing the same kinds of suffering. And after you have suffered for a little while, the God of all grace, who has called you to his eternal glory in Christ, will himself restore, support, strengthen, and establish you. To him be the power forever and ever. Amen. (1 Pet 5:6-11)

A Potpourri of Questions

We enter the sacred chamber on our knees. We still our
thoughts and words, and say, "Lord teach us to pray." Give us
Thy holy desires, and let our prayer be the very echo of Thy will.
A. B. SIMPSON

CONTEMPORARY CULTURE IS GOOD at training us in almost everything and anything . . . except prayer. So a multitude of questions inevitably arise when we become serious about learning to grow in our experience of meditative prayer. You may well have many in your mind right now. Hence, in this chapter I want to work with the most common of these questions.

Can you give a simple, straightforward definition of meditative prayer?

Prayer in general is the interactive communication that transpires between God and ourselves. Meditative prayer in particular is the listening side of this communication.

We are bringing both mind and heart into the presence of God and then we listen to the Lord.

How do I get started if I have never done this before?

I suggest you begin with one verse from the Bible. Say, Psalm 23:1: "The LORD is my shepherd, I shall not want." Read it over prayerfully two or three times and then wait quietly, listening for anything the Lord may want to teach you or any experience God may desire to give you. It is quite straightforward, really. We are simply learning to develop a conversational relationship with God—us talking with God and God talking with us.

Can you share a little about your own experience of meditative prayer?

Right now I am trying something a bit new for me, and to do it I must first find a Bible I have not marked up! I take a short psalm with no more than fifteen verses. Psalm 29 is a good example. I do three readings of the psalm. The first time, I read the psalm out loud to myself, after which I am still for a few moments. On my second reading, I use a felt marking pen and highlight any verses or phrases that speak to my condition. I do this with a prayerful heart trusting that the Lord will focus my attention on what I really need. After the reading I again become completely quiet for a few moments.

On the third reading, I actually do not read the whole psalm but only the passages I have highlighted on the second reading. As I read for the third time, a single verse or phrase often will stand out and that is the passage to which I give my attention. In the case of Psalm 29 the phrase I felt drawn to was "worship the LORD in holy splendor" (29:2). I jot this verse or phrase on a small note card so I can carry it with me throughout the day. But I am not done. Having turned my attention to a particular passage, I sit quietly, listening to the Lord. What am I doing? I am waiting upon the Lord. I am attending to the Lord. I am beholding the Lord. The reading part of my meditation may have taken fifteen minutes, and now the waiting in a listening silence will take perhaps another fifteen minutes. Often I have a cup of coffee with me and slowly sip the coffee as I listen. As with good friends there does not need to be any words. Still, I seek to be attentive to any teaching or experience the Lord wants to bring to me.

I am the mother of a new baby. Is meditative prayer possible for me?

No, not in any ordinary sense. I would say the same to new fathers. New parents are lucky just to make it through the day! And their sleep is constantly interrupted at night. So I suggest you rest easy with yourself. The Lord knows your

heart and understands. After all, God set up the mother-
baby arrangement in the first place. If you are nursing, you
have a lovely image for the transference of life . . . as your
little one is receiving its life from you, you can breathe a
prayer to receive life from the Lord. That is enough. In a
year or two your baby will not need the constant attention
that is now the case, and then you can return to your prayer
practice in a more normal fashion.

Whenever I try to meditate I find myself falling asleep. Any counsel?

It is a sad reality that so many of us live with the emotional spring wound so tightly that the moment we begin
to relieve the tension, sleep overtakes us. The ultimate
answer to this problem is to learn better how to get in
touch with our bodies and our emotions. We need to
learn that fully alert and fully relaxed are completely
compatible states. I find, however, that most of us cannot
learn this in an instant. And so I would suggest if you find
yourself falling asleep when you try to meditate, rather
than chide and condemn yourself, accept the sleep grate-
fully, for no doubt you need it. Besides, as Brother Lawrence has noted, "Those who have been breathed on by
the Holy Spirit move forward even while sleeping." In
time you will discover that the problem will recede into
the background.

Do you have some favorite Bible passages you use for meditation?

I range over the entire Bible: sometimes focusing on personalities in the Old Testament, sometimes on the psalms or the prophets, sometimes on Jesus' acts of compassion, sometimes on Jesus' parables, sometimes on the cross and resurrection, sometimes on the epistles and so forth. I don't have a favorite per se. But let me give you seven passages as a kind of starter kit. You could use one passage each day for a week or, better yet, stay with one passage for a week and then go to the next passage for the second week and so forth, giving you seven weeks of meditation passages. I suggest the seven great "I am" passages of Jesus. Be sure to include the entire passage in your meditation.

1. "I am the bread of life" (John 6:35-40).

2. "I am the light of the world" (John 8:12-20).

3. "I am the gate" (John 10:1-10).

4. "I am the good shepherd" (John 10:11-18).

5. "I am the resurrection and the life" (John 11:17-27).

6. "I am the way, and the truth, and the life" (John 14:1-14).

7. "I am the true vine" (John 15:1-17).

How can I be sure that I am hearing the voice of God?
It is very important to have the answer to this question clear in your mind. Remember, Satan pushes and condemns, God draws and encourages. You can tell the difference. Get clear in your mind the great teaching in the New Testament of the Christlikeness of God . . . God is like Jesus. Then, become intimately familiar with Jesus, first from the Gospel records and then in your personal experience. Cling to the words of Jesus that he is the good Shepherd and that his sheep "know his voice" (Jn 10:4). God will always draw you to what is life-giving, to those things that are true, honest, just, pure, lovely and of a good report (Phil 4:8).

David Pytches in his book *Does God Speak Today?* has compiled stories of people who have received "words" from God, as well as fourteen cases that are pretty clearly mistaken claims of hearing from God. This study will help clarify for you when God is speaking. You may want to review the teaching in chapter six of this book about discerning the voice of God. Then, if any questions remain, share your concern with a friend who is seasoned in the working of the Spirit. Trust me, with a little practice you will become clear when you are hearing the voice of God.

Is it really necessary for me to meditate?
No . . . and yes. You don't need to talk with your parents

in order to be their child. But why wouldn't you? And if you talk with them, wouldn't you also want to listen to what they might want to say? A healthy back-and-forth conversation produces a healthy relationship. The same is true with God. How I wish I could adequately convey to you how much God desires our presence. We have been created for an intimate conversational relationship with God. Just remember the wise counsel of Thomas Merton: "Anyone who imagines he can simply begin meditating without praying for the desire and the grace to do so, will soon give up. But the desire to meditate, and the grace to begin meditating, should be taken as an implicit promise of further graces. In meditation, as in anything else in the Christian life, everything depends on our correspondence with the grace of the Holy Spirit."

When is the best time for meditation?

The answer to this question varies from person to person and often is different for individuals at different points in their life. For example, in my high-school years the morning hour was especially valuable; as a college student a free hour just before lunch met my needs better; in graduate school less frequent but more extended periods were most helpful; and in the middle-age years the morning time again seemed best. You will find your own rhythm. If possible, find the time when your energy level is at its peak and give that, the best of your day, to this sacred work.

Where is the best place for meditation?

To this I want to make three observations. First, every place is sacred in the Lord, and we need to know that wherever we are is holy ground. We are a portable sanctuary and by the power of God we sanctify all places. My second observation is, however, a bit antithetical to the first. Most of us find certain places more conductive to meditative prayer than others. In addition, there do seem to be certain special "thin places" where a sense of the Shekinah of God is especially near. We do well to find a place of beauty that is quiet, comfortable and free from emotional and physical distraction. With a little creativity most of us can arrange such a place with minimal effort.

Third, I have discovered that certain activities are particularly conducive to meditative prayer. Swimming and jogging are singularly appropriate for this interior work. A brisk walk is often enhanced by whispering the Jesus Prayer in tune to your stride . . . "Lord Jesus Christ, Son of God, have mercy on me, a sinner." Some have found gardening a happy time to know "the LORD, who made heaven and earth" (Ps 124:8). For a few years I enjoyed periods of meditation while riding the bus to work; while it takes a little practice to disregard the ordinary commotion, it soon becomes a wonderful place of solitude.

Is one length of time better than another?

For the most part this is a matter of your past experience and internal readiness. Some live so frantically that five or ten minutes of quietness stretches them to the limit. But with a little practice thirty to forty minutes should feel comfortable. Let your own needs and abilities determine your schedule. It is better to take small portions and digest them fully than to attempt to gorge yourself and get spiritual indigestion.

What posture is best?

Again the answer lies in what fits you best . . . with this one qualification. Most of us fail to understand how helpful the body can be in spiritual work. For example, if we feel particularly distracted and out of touch with spiritual things, a consciously chosen posture of kneeling can help call the inner spirit to attention. Romano Guardini points out that the simple Christian act of kneeling is intended as a "discipline of posture, not of comfort." I suggest sitting in a comfortable but straight chair with the back correctly positioned and both feet flat on the floor. Richard Rolle said that in "sitting I am most at rest, and my heart most upward." The hands outstretched or placed on the knees palms up gently nudges the inner mind into a stance of receptivity.

Does meditative prayer exclude an active life?

Oh no. Far from it. William Penn observed, "True Godliness does not turn men out of the world, but enables them to live better in it and excites their endeavors to mend it." The tradition of a life of prayer leading people into the most vigorous active life is long and well documented. Think of St. Patrick hurled by God into Ireland to be the answer to its spiritual poverty. Think of St. Francis thrust into a worldwide ministry of compassion for all people, for all animals, for all creation. Think of Elizabeth Fry driven by divine compassion into the hellhole of Newgate prison, which led to her great work of prison reform. Think of William Wilberforce laboring his entire life for the abolition of the slave trade. Think of William and Catherine Booth serving tirelessly among the homeless of London, which eventually led to the founding of the Salvation Army. Think of Father Damion living and suffering and dying among the lepers of Moloki. Think of Mother Teresa ministering among the poorest of the poor in India and throughout the world. Gordon Cosby has observed, "A time will come when the two emphases—contemplation and action—intersect and become one, for the true contemplative is a man of action."

How does my personal experience of meditative prayer relate to the gathered experience of worship? Or does it?
It does indeed. If only a few individuals have developed an intimate, ongoing conversational relationship with God, it will affect the entire atmosphere of the gathered community. The entertainment show that is so characteristic of contemporary worship will begin to feel plastic and artificial, and people will instinctively seek something deeper, more profound. Nothing needs to be said nor any complaints made. It is the very substance of your life that will have an effect and draw others like a magnet toward Christ. Plus, you are free to simply be with the people in all their loving and frustrating ways.

Are there books you would recommend I read on meditative prayer?
Thomas Merton rightly observed, "You cannot learn meditation from a book. You just have to *meditate*." Now, I am glad you are reading this book, and I hope it is helpful to you. But the purpose of any book on meditation is to get us into the practice of meditation just like a book on the rules for the game of soccer is intended to get us out on the field and into the game. At the back of this book is an appendix with some suggested readings. However, it is important that we not just read but "get into the game."

Should I talk about my meditative experiences to others?
Not much. An oak tree can send a tap root down sixty feet
in search of water, and its tiered root system will permeate
different layers of the soil. Some of these roots will extend
out more than twice the drip line. Yet we will have picnics
under the shade of this giant oak, and our children climb in
its branches without a single thought about the root system
that makes the great tree possible. So for us. The root system of prayer is for the sake of the substance of the life of
the person.

You may remember that Paul had an experience of being
caught up into the third heaven. Were you also aware that it
was fourteen years before he said anything about it? Or that
he spoke of it only because he was pressured to discuss "vi-
sions and revelations"? Or that he refused to speak about what
he learned for he "heard things that are not to be told, that no
mortal is permitted to repeat" (2 Cor 12:1-4)? You see, some
experiences are meant for us alone. Now and again it may be
appropriate to share a little of our experience, but even then
it should be done discreetly and with humility of heart.

QUESTIONS ABOUNDING

You still have many more questions, I'm sure. Me too. It is
good to know that we are not left to our own devices. Jesus
is our present Teacher. He will guide us into what we need
to know when we need to know it.

Entering the Experience

Encounter at Jalama Beach

This, then, is the extravagant landscape of the world, given, given with pizzazz, given in good measure, pressed down, shaken together, and running over.

Annie Dillard

*I*T HAS BEEN A LONG TIME SINCE I have thought of travel as an adventure. Still, this is one trip I am anticipating. The express reason for the trip is to deliver the commencement address at Westmont College in Santa Barbara, California. Westmont's president, Dr. Gayle Beebe, is a former student of mine, and I always feel that any opportunity to be with him is well worth the time and travel. I do have another reason, however.

Whenever possible on business trips I schedule a twenty-four-hour private retreat for my own renewal and spiritual growth. On an earlier trip to Santa Barbara I took a solitary hike in the nearby Channel Islands. This time I am hoping for a daylong prayer walk along a secluded stretch of coastline named Jalama Beach.

❉   ❉   ❉

Once in Santa Barbara I jump into commencement activities with relish. My pattern is always to be as fully present as possible to the people and activities of the moment. When I travel there is no multitasking for me. No cell phone calls. No extraneous interviews. No catching up on e-mail. No laptop computer work in between events. All my energies are focused on the present moment and the precious people filling those moments.

Any commencement setting is abuzz with people and events. A reception for the graduates—all bright and eager and full of promise. Greetings and everyday chitchat with staff and secretaries and food service people—each one so crucial to the functioning of a college. Introductions to dignitaries of one kind and another—each one a unique person with even more unique stories to tell.

I attend the baccalaureate service. With no official part to play I am free to sit among the parents and guests who have come for this auspicious event. I watch them closely, and it is moving to feel their button-popping pride. Many no doubt have waited and hoped for this day for a very long time. Three students share brief reflections—well done, I might add. The main address is by Mark Nelson, Westmont's professor of philosophy. He is obviously a hit with the students, and his talk is a grand-slam home run. In fact, the faculty as a whole impress me no end.

My commencement address the next day is on a topic I am passionate about, "The Humiliation of the Word in our Day." My title was drawn from the famous French writer Jacques Ellul, and I am hoping to give the concept contemporary relevance. My final point has particular application for the ongoing life of contemplative prayer . . . and for my hoped-for retreat the next day:

> Fourth, and finally, I urge you, the class of 2010, to allow your words to be grounded in silence. Remember T. S. Eliot in *Ash Wednesday* when he asked,
>
> > Where shall the word be found
> > where will the word
> > Resound?
> > Not here, there is not enough silence.
>
> You see, distraction is one of the deepest problems we face today. All of the visual stimuli, all of the chatter of the blogosphere, all of the confusion of doublespeak keep us perpetually distracted.
>
> Remember, silence is a spiritual discipline and we need this discipline to unplug us from the inane babble of modern culture. Today, as a result of e-mailing and texting (wonderful technological inventions in themselves), we are saying more and more about less and less. For many this has become a genuine addic-

tion. The din of noisy words tossed out so casually, so superficially, so carelessly snuff out the silence that would open us to the voice of the Spirit that groans within us. So, in our day we must learn to be still. To wait. To hold our tongue. To observe. To ponder. To wonder.

Silence cultivates the soil of our hearts so that life-giving words are allowed to germinate and take root. Then when the time comes for speaking, our words will flow like water from a silent spring.

The day's festivities are rounded off with one gigantic reception on the college lawn for congratulations and pictures and greetings and introductions of relatives from far and wide.

❋   ❋   ❋

Sunday morning, May 9, is my retreat day—Mother's Day. I rise early, buy an apple and a bit of cheese for the day and head out for Jalama Beach. The hills along the narrow, winding fifteen miles of Jalama Road explode with bright yellow mustard plants. There are multiplied millions of these blooms, and they will all be gone once the summer heat gets to them. Amazing.

As I reach the high cliff overlooking the beach, I can see lupine and sunflowers waving in the wind. My mind wanders to the salient words of Agnes Sanford: "The simplest and oldest way, then, in which God manifests Himself is . . . through and in the earth itself. And He still speaks to us through the earth and the sea, the birds of the air and the little living creatures upon the earth, if we can but quiet ourselves to listen."

So today I am here to listen. As I drive into Jalama Beach proper, the park ranger deadpans, "May is our windy month." I soon realize that his words tossed out so casually were a warning. The moment I step onto the beach itself I am greeted by a fierce wind whipping up waves and sand. "At least it will discourage potential beachcombers," I muse.

Rather than face the wind head on I wander over to Jalama Creek and consider its role in providing a ready source of fresh water for the Chumash Indians who lived along this coastline for many centuries. It is easy to see why a substantial village of the Chumash existed here where the creek meets the sea. It was significant enough that the name of the village has survived to the present—Shilimaqsh-tush—but I can find no translation for the name.

I ponder these things as I look out at the giant cattails massed along the creek bank, bending in the wind. I see other plants too; elderberry and nettles and bulrushes. I wonder about these people, at one time eighteen thousand strong, who built a complex society that thrived for centuries. Especially unusual were their "tomel" boats, which enabled them to travel to and populate several of the nearby Channel Islands.

In 2001 a small group of contemporary Chumash re-created that dangerous journey, and now once a year they paddle tomel boats from the mainland to Santa Cruz island to celebrate a culture now all but extinct. The tribal decimation is an old story—the influx of European diseases to which the Chumash people had no immunological resistance. Eventually this entire village was rounded up and transferred to the nearby La Purisima Mission. Shilimaqshtush was no more. By 1900 the number of Chumash people had been reduced to a mere two hundred, although present day estimates are roughly three thousand souls.

I ponder all these things in my heart. The earth itself seems to rise up in protest against the inhumanity of it all. Perhaps that part of my own Ojibway heritage is responding with sadness to all that has transpired on this spot. The California missions no doubt produced many good things, and yet . . . wouldn't the Chumash people have been better served if they had been able to continue living in this lovely coastal spot? I don't know, I just wonder.

※   ※   ※

Christian theology teaches us that there are two major texts for our study and meditation: the Bible and the "book of nature." Today I have come to Jalama Beach with the intention of studying the book of nature to see what the Lord might teach me. Evelyn Underhill reminds us that "to elude nature, to refuse her friendship and attempt to leap the river of life in the hope of finding God on the other side, is the common error of a perverted mysticality. . . . So you are to begin with that first form of contemplation which the old mystics sometimes called the 'discovery of God in His creatures.'"

It is time for me to enter the coastal windy blast directly. I reckon that if John Muir could lash himself to the top of a tree in a Yosemite snowstorm, I should be able to endure a little wind. I'm hoping for an extended prayer walk of five, maybe six hours. So I step out onto the beach proper where for many centuries Chumash children laughed and played and Chumash women cooked and made baskets and Chumash men hunted and fished. What might I learn?

Winds hit me full face and push me back. Blowing sand stings my cheeks and legs. I quickly turn my back to the wind and decide I should walk with the wind rather than against it. Of course, I will eventually need to head back . . . but maybe by then the stinging blast will have died down. I pull my hat tight around my ears, cinching the drawstring under my chin. One thing for sure, I'm the only person foolish enough to be out here. Solitude is mine today.

I remember Jesus' words that the Holy Spirit is rather

like the wind—we do not know where it comes from and we do not know where it goes. So I walk along trying to imagine this wind like the Holy Spirit. But I quickly abandon the metaphor—even the fiery blast of Pentecost could not have been this violent! The wind is just the wind and today I must contend with wind.

Walking with the wind allows me to see things quite well. The blowing sand stings my legs a bit but this is only a small nuisance. I can walk quickly with the wind pushing me along. The ocean waves are churning today; they too are being blown hither and yon. A wondrous, wild beauty.

In the space of half a mile I come across three live starfish stranded on the shore by the wind's turbulence. I toss them back into the churning waves, thinking of the story by Loren Eiseley of the little boy throwing starfish back into the sea. The boy is confronted by someone who points out the hopelessness of his action: Since there are miles and miles of beach and hundreds of starfish, he can't possibly make any difference. The child answers simply, as he tosses another starfish into the sea, "I am making a difference for this starfish." A rather sentimental story really. But today I find it helpful to think of the value of touching just one life for good. I consider how I might be attentive to "that solitary individual," as Kierkegaard put it.

Another mile down the beach I come upon a dead seal washed up on the shore. A recent death, I surmise, for no scavengers have yet descended on the carcass. This is the cruel, ugly violence of nature. But then, maybe not so cruel nor so ugly after all. This is simply the process of life and death that is part of the world in which we live. Still, I am sad at the death of this seal. It causes me to consider the countless number of seals who perish in the ocean every day without anyone to know or care. Except perhaps God.

After an hour of walking I am quite done in by the fierce wind. Its blowing, blowing, blowing is becoming more than a nuisance, more than a bother. It is a sharp pain blocking out all else. I search for some way to escape the wind. The sea cliffs here provide no cave or shelter that I can see. Quickly I jog around a bend in the cliff wall hoping that will shelter me somewhat. No such luck. The wind seems even more ferocious than before. I conclude this just isn't my day for sweet lessons from the book of nature.

Just then I climb over a small rock promontory jutting out into the sand. Normally I wouldn't give it a second look, but today I notice that on the other side a hollow has formed in the rock that is just large enough for me to crawl into. So I do. I am half lying, half sitting inside this rock formation and it is a perfect shelter from the wind. The sand blows past me only inches above my head. I decide to stay awhile.

I examine the rock that covers and protects me. It is nothing like the granite I cherish so much in the Rockies.

Still, it is a good-quality Monterrey chert. I read earlier that the Chumash used this rock to fashion beautifully flaked knives. This hollow in the rock is a perfect place for me to ponder . . . to pray. The sky is an azure blue. Wisps of clouds quickly pass overhead chased by the wind. Looking carefully into the sky I can see the moon, only a sliver this time of the month. In the full light of day it is quite pale. Indeed, I would have never noticed it without my stationary, half-reclining position.

In this little shelter in the rock I am able to pray. "All praise to you Lord God, Creator of all things. The thunder of the waves, the whistle of the wind, even this rock that protects me praises you. So this morning I too lift my heart in praise and thanksgiving."

I think about Jesus who is the Master of wind and wave. I tried earlier in the day to tell the wind to stop and quickly learned that my prayer abilities are definitely not in the "calm-the-wind-and-waves" class. I feel a little like Elijah keeping his lonely vigil over earthquake, wind and fire.

I am content now in my tiny shelter, quietly watching waves crashing against the rock and seagulls struggling against the wind. I munch on my apple and cheese. This is a good place to be. My soul is still. Listening.

※　　※　　※

Rock, however, is completely unyielding. After an hour or

so in my cozy little shelter, my back and butt ache. I need to move. So I rise and face the wind head on. It has not lessened one decimal point. I must make my way back into the full force of the sandy blast. Miserable. But I have no other choice.

On my return I turn my face sideways to protect my nose and eyes somewhat. In this position I observe the cliffs above me more closely than earlier. Nothing unusual really, only the Monterrey chert slowly disintegrating under the force of relentless waves.

But then, high up on the cliff's edge, I see a tall wooden cross. I look at it for a long time as I walk by ever so slowly against the wind. There is no marker. No sign of any kind. It is quite weathered and simple. Only pasture land sprawls out in the hills beyond the cross. Why is it there? Does it mark some tragic accident? Did a child fall from this cliff onto the rocks below? Maybe.

I wonder though if the reason for this weathered cross could be different altogether. Maybe someone just wanted to set into this rugged cliff a reminder of the greatest event in all of history. The Son of God in relentless love hanging on a tree on Golgotha's hillside. I don't know. I just wonder.

※　※　※

I make my way back to the park headquarters, tired and sandy. A little Jalama Beach store and grill is nearby. They feature "the world-famous Jalama Burger," and I order the whole, sloppy mess with all the fixings. No veggie or vegan food for me today!

On the walls of the grill are pictures and stories of the area's history. The wind, I note, has been a wild presence for a long time. On one stormy night in 1923 seven ships broke apart on these rocky shores and twenty-five lives were lost. I conclude that my little skirmish with the wind was only child's play next to what many have experienced on these shores. The Chumash people surely endured many a windy day. What did they do? And what might they say to me?

I eat my Jalama Burger and consider my day. Did the wind defeat me? Perhaps. Certainly it wasn't the day I thought I would have. Did I learn any shattering spiritual lessons from the book of nature? No, but I am content with my experience. Weather of all kinds, physical and spiritual, is all part of our life with God.

A Concluding Word

Since I learned how to enter the forest of meditation, I have received sweet dewlike drops from that forest. I have found that the door to meditation is open everywhere and any time, at midnight or at noonday, at dawn or at dusk. Everywhere, on the street, on the trolley, on the train, in the waiting room, or in a prison cell, I am given a resting place of meditation, wherein I can meditate to my heart's content on the Almighty God who abides in my heart. . . . Those who draw water from the wellspring of meditation know that God dwells close to their hearts. For those who wish to discover the quietude of old amid the hustle and bustle of today's machine civilization, there is no way save to rediscover this ancient realm of meditation. Since the loss of my eyesight I have been as delighted as if I had found a new wellspring by having arrived at this sacred precinct.

TOYOHIKO KAGAWA

THE JOURNEY INTO MEDITATIVE PRAYER is a long one. We may be hesitant and unsure that we even want to take the journey. But in time, something marvelous begins occurring within. Slowly but surely each of us is being changed into the image of Christ. Our hearts' desires begin to be formed in a new direction. Our feelings, our hopes, our longings all begin moving upward, Godward. The good rises up. The evil loses its grip. Our lives are penetrated throughout by love. We feel ourselves going from faith to faith—from the faith we have to the faith that is yet to come. This faith enables us to see more clearly everything in the light of God's overriding governance for good. We feel a seed of hope growing within us, a hope that is able to carry us through the most difficult of circumstances. And a new power is generated deep within, power to overcome evil and to do what is right.

This transforming work does not happen all at once and not completely perhaps. But it does happen. The old games of manipulation and control begin losing their appeal to us. Guile becomes less and less a pattern of our daily life. A new compassion rises up within us for the bruised and the broken and the dispossessed. Indeed, it's a kind of well-reasoned concern for the well-being of all people, of all creation. We are becoming friends of Jesus (Jn 15:14).

We may find ourselves looking at the changes in ourselves with surprised joy. We never thought in our wildest dreams that we would ever want to be a holy person. But now that is exactly what we long for, to be holy in a strong, winsome, vigorous sense. Interactive communication with God is becoming a natural way of life, as is our ability to listen. We are keen to listen for the voice of the true Shepherd. Not always and not perfectly. But the desire and the ability grow with each and every day. Well, not "every" day. But the days we fail to live in lively communion feel empty and wasted. The days of rich fellowship are more full, more satisfying.

We begin this exercise of meditative prayer out of an inner longing, but only as it becomes a holy habit will we stay with it. And the most amazing change of all is we begin living each day under a new power and a new management. We are owned by God and we are responding accordingly. We are learning, in the words of George Fox, to "walk cheerfully over the world."

WELCOME HOME

In the summer of 1990 I was working furiously on what is now *Prayer: Finding the Heart's True Home*. Of course it wasn't a book then, just thousands of scrawled notes on scraps of paper, napkins and anything else I could find. The library staff at the university where I was teaching at the time gave me a special room for my research. They even gave me a key so I could go in anytime day or night.

Over those summer months I imagine I read three hundred books or more in the field of prayer. Classical books. Contemporary books. Books, books, books. My head was swimming with all the debates about prayer and all the definitions of prayer. I learned every jot and tittle of *oratio* and *meditatio* and *contemplatio*. I got so lost in Teresa of Avila's *Interior Castle* that I didn't know which room was which!

I will never forget one specific night in July 1990. I was in the library all alone. Everyone had left hours ago. It was late. I had read too much, studied too much. I was experiencing overload. How in one book could anyone contend with all of the difficulties and all of the intricacies of prayer? There was no way. I threw up my hands, ready to abandon the project. Then something happened to me. Something that even today I find difficult to explain.

The only way I know to say it is that I saw something. What I saw was the heart of God, and the heart of God was an open wound of love. Then I heard the voice of the true Shepherd, not outwardly but inwardly, saying, "I do not want you to abandon this project. Instead, tell my people, tell my children, that my heart is broken. Their distance and their preoccupation wound me. Tell them. Tell my children to come home."

And so I am telling you. As best I can, I am telling you that God is welcoming you and God is welcoming me home, home to where we belong, home to that for which we were created. We have been in a far country. It has been a country of climb and push and shove. It has been a country of noise and hurry and crowds. And God is welcoming us home—home to peace and serenity and joy.

We need not be afraid. God's arms are stretched out wide to take us in. God's heart is large enough to receive us. Welcome to the living room of God's love, where we can put on old slippers and share freely. Welcome to the kitchen of God's friendship, where chatter and batter mix in good fun. Welcome to the dining room of God's strength, where we can feast to our heart's delight. Welcome to the study of God's wisdom, where we can grow and stretch and ask all the questions we want. Welcome to the workshop of God's creativity, where we become co-laborers with God. Welcome to the bedroom of God's rest, where new peace is found.

Jesus is the doorway into this home that is the heart of God, and prayer is the key that "by grace . . . through faith" unlocks the door (Eph 2:8). Welcome home. Welcome to the sanctuary of the soul.

Acknowledgments

WE ALWAYS STAND ON THE SHOULDERS of those who have gone before us. The debt only increases when we attempt to put ideas into print. I have sought to express something of that debt in the references and endnotes for this book. That, of course, only hints at the writers and thinkers and prayers who have taught me over many years. Most of them belong to earlier centuries, but I still thank them.

Special appreciation goes to my personal assistant, Lynda Graybeal, who read the entire manuscript as it was being written and made helpful comments and corrections. I want to thank Howard Macy, Nathan Foster, Robert Bolton and Gayle Beebe for helping me track down the sources for various quotations. I thank Terri Taylor for providing details of the Quaker Meadow chapel that I had long ago forgotten. I want to express appreciation to Cindy Bunch, senior editor at InterVarsity Press who originally proposed the idea for this book and took keen interest in its development. Then too, I want to thank all those who showed prayerful concern for this project, and for me, from the first day of writing right up to the end.

Finally, I feel a deep debt to Carolynn, my wife. Throughout the days and nights of writing, Carolynn kept encouraging me, prodding me and engaging in vigorous debate with me over particular words and phrases. She brought to the project a wonderful combination of loving and frustrating tenaciousness. She is the love of my life.

Resource Books for Your Journey

I WOULD COUNSEL YOU AGAINST doing a Google search for "books on meditation." The vast majority of the contemporary literature out there is simply a wild goose chase of the blind leading the blind. It is a positive virtue to be ignorant of most of these writings. If you will focus your energies on the classic Christian texts on the subject, you will have a much better chance of making progress in meditative prayer. Below are twelve of the better known and most reliable sources. Of course, most of these authors have written other works beyond the one I mention. I have listed these authors chronologically, and their works can be found in various editions.

Julian of Norwich (1342-1416), *Showings*

Teresa of Avila (1515-1582), *The Interior Castle*

Brother Lawrence of the Resurrection (1614-1691), *The Practice of the Presence of God*

Madame Guyon (1648-1717), *Experiencing the Depths of Jesus Christ*

Jean-Pierre de Caussade (1675-1751), *Self-Abandonment to Divine Providence*

Jean-Nicholas Grou (1730-1803), *How to Pray*

Ole Hallesby (1879-1961), *Prayer*

Frank Laubach (1884-1970), *Letters by a Modern Mystic*

Sadhu Sundar Singh (1889-?), *At the Master's Feet*

Catherine de Hueck Doherty (1896-1985), *Poustinia*

A. W. Tozer (1897-1963), *The Pursuit of God*

Thomas Merton (1915-1968), *Spiritual Direction and Meditation*

Notes

A Beginning Word

page 9 "Meditation is the tongue": As quoted in Richard J. Foster, *Prayer: Finding the Heart's True Home* (San Francisco: Harper-SanFrancisco, 1992), p. 143.

Part One: Laying the Foundation

page 13 "Teach me to stop": Ken Medema, "Teach Me to Stop," *Teach Me to Stop (and Listen)* (Waco, Tex.: Word Music, 1978).

Chapter 1: God Speaking, Teaching and Acting

page 15 "As fundamental a step": Elizabeth O'Connor, *Search for Silence* (Waco, Tex.: Word, 1972), p. 118.

page 20 "Old Testament meditation": Ken A. Bryson, "Silence and Hebrew Meditation" <www.biblicaltheology.com/Research/BrysonKA01.pdf>.

page 21 "Move over, Elijah": For an imaginative and poetic rendering of the story, see Arthur O. Roberts, *Move Over Elijah* (Newberg, Ore.: Barclay, 1967).

page 23 "Breathe through the heat": John Greenleaf Whittier, "Dear Lord and Father of Mankind," *Hymns for the Family of God* (Nashville: Paragon House, 1976), p. 422.

page 23 "Our communicating Cosmos": Dallas Willard, *Hearing God: Developing a Conversational Relationship with God* (Downers Grove, Ill.: InterVarsity Press, 1999), p. 63.

page 24   "Live in his presence": Madame Jeanne Guyon, *Experiencing the Depths of Jesus Christ* (Goleta, Calif.: Christian Books, 1975), p. 3.

page 24   "To pray is to descend": Theophan the Recluse, *The Art of Prayer: An Orthodox Anthology*, ed. Timothy Ware (London: Faber & Faber, 1966), p. 110.

page 24   "Because I am a Christian": Dietrich Bonhoeffer, *The Way to Freedom* (New York: Harper & Row, 1966), p. 57.

page 24   "The depths of Jesus": Guyon, *Experiencing the Depths,* p. 32.

Chapter 2: A Familiar Friendship with Jesus

page 25   "True silence is a key": Catherine de Haeck Doherty, *Poustinia: Christian Spirituality of the East for Western Man* (Notre Dame, Ind.: Ave Maria, 1983), p. 21.

page 25   "A familiar friendship": Thomas à Kempis, *The Imitation of Christ* (Garden City, N.Y.: Image, 1955), p. 85.

page 27   "O my Lord, since it seems": *The Prayers of Teresa of Avila*, ed. Thomas Alvarez (Hyde Park, N.Y.: New City, 1995), p. 12. I have changed the last phrase of this quote slightly for ease of understanding. The text (which, of course, we are getting via translation) reads, "Don't you think it would be good . . . if the inn where You have so continually to dwell were not to get so dirty."

page 27   "Greatest difficulty in conversion": John Flavel, *On Keeping the Heart*, Christian Classics Ethereal Library <www.ccel.org/ccel/flavel/keeping.ii.i.html>.

page 31   "An intolerable scramble": Thomas R. Kelly, *A Testament of Devotion* (San Francisco: HarperSanFrancisco, 1969), p. 100.

page 31   "Unhappy, uneasy": Ibid., p. 92.

pages 31-32   "The divine Center": Ibid., p. 3.

page 32   "This is not ecstasy": Ibid., p. 15.

pages 32-33   "A life of unhurried peace": Ibid., p. 100.

Chapter 3: Descending with the Mind into the Heart

page 34   "The masters of the spiritual life": Romano Guardini, *Prayer in Practice*, trans. Prince Leopold (Garden City, N.Y.: Image, 1963), p. 102.

page 35   "To pray is to descend": Theophan the Recluse, *The Art of Prayer: An Orthodox Anthology*, ed. Timothy Ware (London: Faber & Faber, 1966), p. 110.

page 36   "The divine offices": Alexander Whyte, *Lord, Teach Us to Pray* (New York: Harper & Brothers, n.d.), p. 249.

page 36   "This was my method": Teresa of Avila, *The Complete Works of Saint Teresa of Jesus,* trans. E. Allison Peers (New York: Sheed & Ward, 1949), 1:9.4; see also 4.10.

page 36   "By means of the imagination": Francis de Sales, *Introduction to the Devout Life,* trans. John K. Ryan (Garden City, N.Y.: Image, 1955) p. 84.

page 37   "I long to see the imagination": A. W. Tozer, "The Value of the Sanctified Imagination" <http://loves55houme.com/Books/BAM22.htm>.

page 39   "An affirmation of the Chalcedonian doctrine": As quoted in Richard J. Foster, *Streams of Living Water* (San Francisco: HarperSanFrancisco, 1998) p. 324. For a brief description of the seven ecumenical councils, see pp. 277-81.

page 41   "Represent to your imagination": Francis de Sales, *Introduction*, p. 83.

page 41   "With your imagination anointed": Whyte, *Lord, Teach Us*, p. 251.

Entering the Experience: Worship at Quaker Meadow

page 46   "When I came into the silent assemblies": *Barclay's Apology in Modern English*, ed. Dean Freiday (Manasquan, N.J.: Sowers, 1980), p. 254.

page 51   "Gathered deep in the spirit of worship": Thomas Kelly, *The*

Eternal Promise (New York: Harper & Row, 1966), pp. 82-83.

page 52   "Mind that which is eternal": George Fox as quoted in Kelly, *Eternal Promise*, p. 79.

page 52   "Therefore brethren, let us be careful": William Penn, "Preface to the Journal of George Fox," *A Journal* (1831), posted on The Missing Cross to Purity <www.hallvworthington.com/wjournal/journalintro2.html>.

page 53   "When assembled, it should be": Robert Barclay, *Barclay's Apology*, p. 248.

page 55   "An inward travail and wrestling": Ibid., pp. 248, 256.

page 56   "Prayer . . . is the raising": Karl Rahner, *On Prayer* (New York: Paulist, 1965), p. 7.

Part Two: Stepping into Meditative Prayer

page 57   "He himself is my contemplation": Isaac of Stella as quoted in *The Lord of the Journey: A Reader in Christian Spirituality*, ed. Roger Pooley and Philip Seddon (London: Collins Liturgical, 1986), p. 36.

Chapter 4: Being Present Where We Are

page 59   "The price of true recollection": Thomas Merton, *Spiritual Direction and Meditation* (Collegeville, Minn.: Liturgical, 1960), p. 69.

page 60   "Only to sit and think of God": Frederick W. Faber as quoted in A. W. Tozer, *The Knowledge of the Holy* (San Francisco: Harper & Row, 1961), p. 12.

page 60   "In Recollection": Evelyn Underhill, *Mysticism* (New York: Meridian, 1955), p. 314.

page 61   "The first quarter of an hour": Evelyn Underhill, *Practical Mysticism* (New York: E. P. Dutton, 1943), p. 52.

page 61   "Prayer must begin": Romano Guardini, *Prayer in Practice*, trans. Prince Leopold (New York: Doubleday, 1963), pp. 20-21.

page 62   "Self-abandonment to divine Providence": Jean-Pierre de
                 Caussade, *Self-Abandonment to Divine Providence*, various edi-
                 tions. Sometimes this book is also titled *The Sacrament of the
                 Present Moment.*

page 64   "Pray for me": Mother Teresa, *Major Addresses Delivered at the
                 Conference on Faith and Learning* (North Newton, Kans.: Bethel
                 College, 1980), pp. 85-86.

page 64   "Not God, but you": Søren Kierkegaard, *Purity of Heart Is to
                 Will One Thing,* trans. Douglas V. Steere (New York: Harper
                 & Brothers, 1938), p. 51.

page 65   "Confession has to do with": N. Gordon Cosby, in Elizabeth
                 O'Connor, *Search for Silence* (Waco, Tex.: Word, 1972), p. 12.

Chapter 5: Beholding the Lord

page 69   "The best contemplative tradition": Hans Urs von Balthasar,
                 Prayer (San Francisco: Ignatius, 1986), p. 28.

page 70   "My brother is mad!" Richard Rolle, *The Fire of Love*, trans.
                 Clifton Wolters (New York: Penguin, 1981), p. 13.

page 70   "Of such sincerity and beauty": Ibid., pp. 13-14.

page 70   "It was real warmth": Ibid., p. 45.

page 70   "I was absolutely delighted": Ibid., p. 45.

page 71   "The pause should be": Jeanne Guyon, *Experiencing the Depths
                 of Jesus Christ* (Goleta, Calif.: Christian, 1981), p. 10.

page 72   "Yes, by faith": Ibid., pp. 10-11.

page 72   "Instead, sweetly and silently": Ibid., p. 11.

page 73   "In this very peaceful state": Ibid., p. 11.

page 74   "Earth's crammed with Heaven": Elizabeth Barrett Browning,
                 Aurora Leigh (London: J. Miller, 1864), posted on A Celebra-
                 tion of Women Writers, University of Pennsylvania <digital
                 .library.upenn.edu/women/barrett/aurora/aurora.html>.

pages 76-77   "The prayer of quiet": Teresa of Avila, *The Interior Castle*,
                 trans. Kieran Kavanaugh and Otilio Rodriguez (New York:
                 Paulist, 1979), p. 73 and many other places.

page 77   "Wondrous, terrible, gentle": Catherine de Haeck Doherty, *Poustinia: Christian Spirituality of the East for Western Man* (Notre Dame, Ind.: Ave Maria, 1983), p. 216.

Chapter 6: An Inward Attentiveness

page 78   "Be silent, and listen": François Fénelon as quoted in Richard J. Foster, *Prayer: Finding the Heart's True Home* (San Francisco: HarperSanFrancisco, 1992), p. 163.

page 80   "A filial bond": Edward John Carnell, *Christian Commitment: An Apologetic* (New York: Macmillan, 1957), p. 273 and numerous other places.

page 81   "Certain factors distinguish": Dallas Willard, *Hearing God: Developing a Conversational Relationship with God* (Downers Grove, Ill.: InterVarsity Press, 1999), p. 174.

page 81   "The quality of God's voice": Ibid., p. 175.

page 81   "The inner voice of God": E. Stanley Jones, *A Song of Ascents* (Nashville: Abingdon, 1979), p. 190.

page 81   "Is a spirit of exalted peacefulness": Willard, *Hearing God*, p. 177.

page 82   "The content of a word": Ibid., p. 178.

page 84   "Mr. Creator, why": The official history from the George Washington Carver Monument says that Carver told this story many times in numerous versions. One online source is "George Washington Carver," Jesus Christ Saves Ministries <www.michaelnewdow.com/GeorgeWashingtonCarver.htm>.

pages 85-86   "This has been a week": Frank C. Laubach, *Letters by a Modern Mystic* (Colorado Springs: Purposeful Design, 2007), p. 30.

page 86   "The time of business": Brother Lawrence, *The Practice of the Presence of God* (Old Tappan, N.J.: Revell, 1985), p. 9.

Entering the Experience: Trek to Cuthbert's Cave

page 87   "O my divine Master": Jean-Nicholas Grou, *How to Pray*, trans.

Joseph Dalby (Cambridge, U.K.: James Clarke, 1982), p. 23.

page 97   "Give me": Dag Hammarskjöld, *Markings*, trans. Leif Sjöberg
                 and W. H. Auden (New York: Ballantine, 1993), p. 83.

Part Three: Dealing with Everyday Difficulties

page 101   "Be still my soul!" Katharina von Sclegel, "Be Still My Soul," in
                 Hymns for the Family of God (Nashville: Paragon House, 1976),
                 p. 77.

Chapter 7: Wandering Minds

page 103   "At this very moment": Evelyn Underhill, *Practical Mysticism*
                 (New York: E. P. Dutton, 1915), pp. 37-38.

page 103   "We will be swimming": Sven Birkerts, *The Gutenberg Elegies:
                 The Fate of Reading in an Electronic Age* (New York: Farrar,
                 Straus & Giroux, 1994), p. 193.

page 104   Neuroscience studies: See Nicholas Carr, *The Shallows: What
                 the Internet Is Doing to Our Brains* (New York: W. W. Norton,
                 2010). If you are interested, you might also want to look at
                 Eric R. Kandel, *In Search of Memory: The Emergence of a New Sci-
                 ence of Mind*; Norman Doidge, *The Brain That Changes Itself*; and
                 David J. Buller, *Adapting Minds*.

page 104   "The sole cause": Blaise Pascal, *The Pensées*, trans. Thomas
                 Krailsheimer (New York: Penguin, 1965), p. 37.

page 105   "The first thing to remember": Dietrich Bonhoeffer, *The Way
                 to Freedom* (New York: Harper & Row, 1966), pp. 60-61.

page 107   "Two roads diverged": Robert Frost, "The Road not Taken,"
                 Mountain Interval, various editions.

page 108   "No man is an island": John Donne, Meditation 17, various
                 editions.

page 108   "Batter my heart": John Donne, Holy Sonnet 14, various edi-
                 tions.

page 109   "If as a Flower": George Herbert, *The Temple*, various editions.

page 109   "Yellow flames flutter": Robert Siegel, *A Pentecost of Finches* (Brewster, Mass.: Paraclete, 2006), p. 68. Other poetry books by Robert Siegel include *In a Pig's Eye* and *The Waters Under the Earth*.

page 111   "God does not cease": François Fénelon, *Christian Perfection* (Minneapolis: Bethany House, 1975), pp. 155-56.

Chapter 8: Like A Roaring Lion

page 112   "There are two equal": C. S. Lewis, *The Screwtape Letters* (New York: Macmillan, 1980), p. 3.

page 113   "Satan, the leader": Ibid., p. vii.

page 120   "Circle me, Lord": *Celtic Daily Prayer* (San Francisco: Harper-SanFrancisco, 2002), p. 33. This prayer of protection is taken from the Aidan Compline.

Chapter 9: A Potpourri of Questions

page 123   "We enter the sacred chamber": A. B. Simpson, *The Life of Prayer* (Harrisburg, Penn.: Christian, 1967), p. 9.

page 126   "Those who have been breathed on": Brother Lawrence, *The Practice of the Presence of God*, trans. John J. Delaney (New York: Doubleday, 1977), p. 57.

page 128   David Pytches in his book: David Pytches, *Does God Speak Today?* (Minneapolis: Bethany House, 1989).

page 129   "Anyone who imagines": Thomas Merton, *Spiritual Direction and Meditation* (Collegeville, Minn.: Liturgical, 1960), p. 98.

page 131   "Discipline of posture": Romano Guardini as quoted in Elizabeth O'Connor, *Search for Silence* (Waco, Tex.: Word, 1972), p. 127.

page 131   "Sitting I am most at rest": Richard Rolle as quoted in Merton, *Spiritual Direction*, p. 75.

page 132   "True Godliness does not turn": William Penn, *No Cross, No Crown*, ed. Ronald Selleck (Richmond, Ind.: Friends United Meeting, 1981), p. xii.

page 132   "A time will come": N. Gordon Cosby, in Elizabeth O'Connor, *Search for Silence* (Waco, Tex.: Word, 1972), p. 12.

page 133   "You cannot learn meditation": Merton, *Spiritual Direction*, p. ii.

Entering the Experience: Encounter at Jalama Beach

page 135   "This, then, is the extravagant landscape": Annie Dillard, *Pilgrim at Tinker Creek* (New York: HarperCollins, 1974), p. 148.

page 137   My title was drawn: Jacques Ellul, *The Humiliation of the Word*, trans. Joyce Main Hanks (Grand Rapids: Eerdmans, 1985).

pages 137-38   "Fourth, and finally": Richard J. Foster, "The Humiliation of the Word in Our Day," *Westmont* 30, no. 3 (2010): 13.

page 139   "The simplest and oldest way": Agnes Sanford, *The Healing Gifts of the Spirit* (New York: Lippincott, 1966), p. 25.

page 141   "To elude nature": Evelyn Underhill, *Practical Mysticism* (New York: E. P. Dutton, 1943), pp. 90-91.

A Concluding Word

page 147   "Since I learned how": Toyohiko Kagawa, *Meditations*, trans. Jiro Takenaka (New York: Harper & Brothers, 1950), p. 1.

pages 147-48   "We may be hesitant": There is a certain wisdom in the hesitancy. Meditative prayer does not function on its own. It is intimately connected to the entire range of the classical disciplines of the spiritual life. We must be prepared to enter into the "costly grace" of an overall life of discipleship to Jesus. To learn more about the spiritual disciplines and how they function in a fully orbed spiritual life, see Dallas Willard, *The Spirit of the Disciplines* (San Francisco: Harper & Row, 1988), and Richard J. Foster, *Celebration of Discipline* (San Francisco: HarperSanFrancisco, 1988).

page 149   "Walk cheerfully over the world": George Fox, *The Journal of George Fox*, ed. John L. Nickalls (Cambridge: Cambridge University Press, 1952), p. 263.